HARDBALL ADVOCACY

SECRETS OF THE LOBBY

HENRY C. KYLE III, MPA, CAE

ILLUMIFY
MEDIA.COM

Hardball Advocacy

Published by
Illumify Media Global
www.IllumifyMedia.com
"Let's bring your book to life!"

Paperback ISBN: 978-1-964251-38-7

Cover design by Debbie Lewis
Author photographs by Edwin Demafiles

Printed in the United States of America

Praise for *Hardball Advocacy*

"It's been a pleasure working with Corky since I took over at CSAE, and he has a long-standing reputation among our association community! Corky is a professional with a clear passion for public policy. Those who have—or will—be working with him will have a great experience learning and managing complex legislative and regulatory issues."

Su Hawk, Executive Director,
Colorado Society of Association Executives

———

"I've had the pleasure of knowing and working with Corky Kyle for years, and I can say without hesitation that he is an expert in state lobbying. With over forty-three years of experience representing major clients like The Ford Motor Company and CNA Insurance, Corky brings unmatched knowledge, strategic insight, and a calm, steady hand to every situation. What stands out most, though, is his genuine commitment to mentoring others and sharing his wisdom. Whether navigating complex legislative issues or teaching the next generation of advocates, Corky does it all with professionalism, integrity, and a passion for making a difference."

Kevin J. Grantham, Fremont County Commissioner and
Former President of the Colorado Senate

"I have had the privilege of knowing and working with Corky. His forty-four years of state lobbying experience speaks volumes about his deep understanding of the legislative process and ability to deliver results. Throughout his distinguished career, Corky has successfully represented major clients, such as the Colorado Society of Association Executives and the Independent Insurance Agents of Colorado. His strategic thinking and relationship-building skills have made him a trusted advocate across various industries, consistently ensuring that his client's legislative and regulatory goals are met precisely and effectively.

"In addition to his direct lobbying work, Corky has been a dedicated educator and mentor, sharing his knowledge with the next generation of advocacy professionals. His commitment to fostering excellence in the state lobbying and advocacy programming has left a lasting impact on many in the field, ensuring that ethical and effective advocacy continues to thrive.

"Whether working in the legislative arena or guiding others in their careers, Corky exemplifies professionalism, expertise, and a passion for shaping sound public policy, enhancing the accountability and transparency of state government."

Mike Coffman, Mayor, City of Aurora, Colorado

———

"Part business, part personal experience, *Hardball Advocacy: Secrets of the Lobby*, is full of practical ways to jumpstart your legislative experience"

Tracy Kraft Tharp, Former Jefferson County Commissioner and Former State Representative

———

"If you've ever wondered how policy really gets made, *Hardball Advocacy* is the book for you. Corky pulls back the curtain on the lobbying world, sharing the strategies and the stories that drive results. This book is an invaluable resource for anyone wanting to understand or engage in the hard-hitting world of advocacy."

Bill Owens, Former Governor of Colorado

———

"Corky Kyle is a master lobbyist who's worked with legislators and his clients from pay phone calls at the capital to Zoom meetings anywhere, anytime. His expertise is relationships – how to build them and how to keep them no matter how the legislature looks by party or legislators. His title is *Hardball Advocacy,* because the stakes are large, but he knows when to pitch a softball if that's how to get work done. It's a complicated game with twists and turns, but Corky gives the insights to how to play the game fair, square, and win."

Paula Noonan, President and Owner of Capitol Watch

———

"It is my pleasure to endorse Corky Kyle, a seasoned and highly respected professional in lobbying and association management. With over forty-four years of experience working with businesses, associations, and public entities, Corky has built a solid reputation for his expertise, integrity, and tireless advocacy.

"As a lobbyist, Corky brings a rare blend of compassion and hands-on experience to the table. He has a well-rounded understanding of the legislative process and an innate knowledge of how associations function and what it takes to drive impactful advocacy efforts.

"Corky is not only an exceptional advocate for his clients; his focus on service excellence ensures that every client is supported at every step."

Julie McCluski, Speaker of the House,
Colorado House of Representatives.

Contents

Acknowledgments

There are many people who have shaped my life, my career, and my passion for advocacy. I'm grateful to everyone listed below.

To my loving wife, Susan Kyle, whose constant support and encouragement have been my foundation, thank you for putting up with my long hours; to my children, Jeff, Kristen, Brandon, and Cody, and their families, thank you for filling my life with pride and joy; to my sister, Karen Daugherty, whose love and presence have been a cherished part of my journey; and to my parents, Lois and Henry Kyle, thank you for teaching me the values of hard work, integrity, and perseverance.

To the mentors and life influencers who left an indelible mark on me: Mr. John Harvill, my High School football coach, who instilled in me the discipline and determination to succeed; Mr. Fisher, a mentor whose wisdom shaped my path; and Dr. Ron Averyt, my college political science professor, who inspired me to think critically and push boundaries.

To my lifelong friends, Tom Burdette and Bobby Kidwell, whose friendship has been a source of strength and laughter over the years. To my professional colleagues and friends—Robin Dyche, Rich Forsberg, Robert Wilson, Joan Tezak, Don Nabity, Jean McEvoy, Marnie

Biln, Rich Lemon, Dr. Gordon Rheaume, and Sarah Heaton—your collaboration and camaraderie have enriched my career.

To my exceptional book team: Emma Seel, Emma DeStefano Holly Duckworth, Tim Jackson, Jenn Clark, Publisher Michael Klassen, photographer Ed Demafiles and Copyeditor Geoff Stone—your expertise and dedication made this project possible.

To my clients over the years, whose trust and partnerships have allowed me to do the work I love, and to the many legislators and staff members I've had the privilege to work alongside—thank you for the opportunity to engage in this important and meaningful profession.

This book is a reflection of all you have given me, and I am forever grateful.

Introduction

"A lobbyist is the person you hire to protect you
from the people you elect."

I n the dynamic and often misunderstood world of political advocacy, the line between influence and manipulation, persuasion and
coercion usually blurs. *Hardball Advocacy: Secrets of the Lobby* by
Henry C. Kyle III (Corky for short) is a bold and unflinching dive
into the heart of this complex and captivating realm.

This book arrives at a critical juncture in our political discourse.
In an era where transparency is demanded yet rarely delivered, Corky
opens the door to a world many suspect, but few truly understand.
It's a world where the stakes are high, the players are savvy, and the
rules are written and rewritten behind closed doors.

What makes *Hardball Advocacy* stand out is its unapologetic
honesty about the tactics and strategies employed in the halls of power and its deep understanding of such actions' ethical, legal, and social
implications. Corky navigates these complex waters with the skill of

a seasoned lobbyist and the clarity of a thought leader in political strategy.

Hardball Advocacy is meticulously researched, drawing on Corky's extensive experience in the field, interviews, case studies, and real-world scenarios. This isn't just a theoretical exploration; it's a practical guide that reveals the mechanics of lobbying, the art of persuasion, and the often-invisible forces that shape policy and political fortunes.

For political science students, lobbying practitioners, or anyone intrigued by the intersection of power, policy, and persuasion, *Hardball Advocacy* is an essential read. It challenges preconceived notions, poses complex ethical questions, and provides insights that are both enlightening and, at times, unsettling.

As you turn these pages, prepare to be taken on a journey through the corridors of power, to see the levers of policymaking up close, and to gain a deeper understanding of the delicate balance between advocacy and influence. *Hardball Advocacy: Secrets of the Lobby* is more than just a book; it is a revealing lens into a world that shapes our lives in ways we often don't see.

Chapter 1: **Three Pivotal Moments**

"But I have promises to keep,
And miles to go before I sleep,
And miles to go before I sleep."

— Robert Frost,
"Stopping by Woods on a Snowy Evening"

have always been a proactive person. I have not been one to go along for the ride. I have been active in pursuing my ideas and goals. I am a person who makes things happen. When there is a problem, I don't let myself be intimidated. I find a solution and work it. This is how I got into lobbying. I had a public policy issue pop up that adversely affect my association. I had to react, so I jumped into the legislative process.

Most people don't set out to become a lobbyist. There aren't degrees in lobbying. For me there were three pivotal moments that led to my becoming a lobbyist.

First Event

My first exposure to the political process came when I was seventeen in my hometown of Gaithersburg, Maryland. My girlfriend's father, Mr. Fisher, was an avid hunter. He invited me to testify alongside him before the Montgomery County Commissioners on a local hunting issue. Nervously, I stood in front of the officials and delivered my testimony, which lasted a whole two minutes. Although brief, it was my first taste of public speaking at a hearing—a moment that sparked my interest in civic engagement, though I didn't fully realize it then.

A couple years later, I cast my first vote while studying at Lincoln College at Oxford University during my senior year. I voted by mail-in ballot from my small, cramped room. The room had no central heating; I fed 50 pence into a heater for every half-hour of warmth. Despite the discomfort, it was a significant moment. Sitting there, I filled out my ballot and voted for Richard Nixon. It wasn't the most glamorous of settings, but it marked my first formal participation in the democratic process.

Second Event

After returning to the U.S., I graduated from Ottawa University in Kansas with a degree in political science. My advisor, Dr. Ronnie Averyt, was a crusty but brilliant professor with a knack for making political science come alive. His passion for politics ignited a similar spark in me. He convinced me that political engagement was not just exciting but necessary—and though I didn't know it then, the seed was planted for me to become a lobbyist.

A few years after earning my undergraduate degree and moving back to Maryland, I felt drawn toward public service and decided to pursue graduate studies. I applied to several programs and was accepted into the University of New Mexico public administration program. My wife and I packed everything we owned, loaded it into a Ryder truck, and headed West. Two years later, I had my master's degree and began working for the Albuquerque Board of Realtors. Little did I know, this was the beginning of a new chapter that would lay the foundation for my political career.

Third Event

Working at the Albuquerque Board of Realtors immersed me in local politics. The executive of the board, Max Mansur, was a seasoned Realtor who had retired from real estate to focus on political advocacy. Over the five years we worked together, I watched closely as he deftly navigated the political landscape, representing the real estate industry before the city council. He used his relationships with elected officials to communicate issues effectively, and his ability to manage testimony and present information to protect property rights was nothing short of remarkable. Watching him operate, I learned the art of local political advocacy and began building my foundation for a career in lobbying.

In 1981, I was hired as the executive vice president of the Independent Insurance Agents of Colorado. My mentor, Don Nabity, the retiring executive, was deeply involved in property and casualty insurance issues. He had a wealth of experience representing the association before the Colorado legislature and the state's insurance department, and he introduced me to both the legislative and regulatory arenas. Don taught me how to work with legislators—how to build relationships, develop strategies, and provide the correct information to influence decision-making.

The regulatory side of politics was an entirely different beast. While legislators are elected and responsive to their constituents, regulators are appointed officials whose job is to interpret legislation and implement policy through rules and regulations. Many regulators knew little about the industries they were tasked with overseeing, and Don taught me how to approach these individuals with a different strategy: one that focused on educating and influencing through careful communication and relationship-building. These lessons in working with both legislators and regulators were invaluable.

I managed the Independent Insurance Agents of Colorado for eleven years, until the association decided it was time for new leadership in 1992. Getting fired was a blow to my ego and my sense of self-worth. I was devastated—shocked, lost, and unsure of my future. For a time, I felt like flotsam, drifting aimlessly. But as it turned out, this event signaled a new beginning.

Two weeks after being fired, I founded The Kyle Group, a lobbying firm that would become my professional home for decades. In hindsight, this difficult moment was the push I needed to follow my true calling as a professional lobbyist. I learned that sometimes the toughest challenges open the door to our most incredible opportunities. Events unfold for a reason, shaping our destiny in ways we don't always see at first. Lesson learned.

After decades in this field, I'm excited to share my knowledge and experience with you. Whether you aspire to be a lobbyist or an engaged activist, I'll help you learn how to navigate the political process, manage government relations, and hold your elected officials accountable and transparent.

> "Politics is the art of looking for trouble, finding it everywhere, diagnosing it incorrectly, and applying the wrong remedies."
>
> — Ernest Benn

Chapter 2: So, You Want to Know a Lobbyist?

"Lobbyists and advocates play a crucial role in the legislative process by serving as intermediaries between lawmakers and various interest groups. They provide expert knowledge, craft persuasive arguments, and help legislators understand the real-world impacts of proposed policies. Effective lobbying ensures that diverse voices are heard and that legislators are informed as they make decisions."

—Thomas Hale

My experience in advocacy began with my work in association management as the executive vice president and lobbyist for Colorado's property and casualty insurance agents, who were members of the Independent Insurance Agents of Colorado. In this role, I represented their interests on key issues like workers' compensation, auto insurance, and property insurance at both the legislative and regulatory levels. One of my proudest achievements was the passage of the continuing education bill for licensed insurance agents. It was the first bill I ever drafted, and I guided it through every step of the process—finding sponsors, building support, navigating committees, and ultimately seeing it signed into law by the governor. That experience was more than just a professional milestone; it showed me the power of persistence, collaboration, and the ability of advocacy to shape policies that directly impact people's lives.

So, what am I—a lobbyist or an advocate? In truth, I am both. A lobbyist works to influence policy on behalf of clients, while an advocate seeks to champion causes and enact meaningful change. For me, these roles are inseparable. As a lobbyist, I represent my clients with integrity and determination, but as an advocate, I approach the work with a deep sense of purpose—focused on finding solutions, building relationships, and improving systems for the better. Whether drafting legislation, collaborating with lawmakers, or testifying before committees, I have always believed that the heart of this profession lies not in power or persuasion but in fostering trust, solving problems, and delivering results that serve the greater good.

In this chapter you will learn

- What is an advocate?
- What is a lobbyist?
- The roles of both in the political process.
- What makes a person an excellent advocate or lobbyist?
- Personal qualities of an advocate and lobbyist.
- Do you have what it takes to do the job?

So, your journey begins. Starting now, I will introduce you to the world of political activism. You will learn the nuances of being an advocate or a lobbyist, exploring why these roles exist, their ethical boundaries, and the skills required to excel. Let's begin with a question: Are you an advocate or a lobbyist?

Advocate

An advocate supports, defends, or argues on behalf of others, typically focusing on broader social, political, or economic issues. They may work for non-profit organizations, advocacy groups, or as individuals committed to a cause. Advocates are driven by a desire to bring about change or justice and engage in activities like public campaigning, education, and raising awareness. Advocacy is not confined to professional roles; it can be pursued by anyone passionate about a cause.

Lobbyist

A lobbyist is usually employed by a specific entity, such as a corporation, industry group, or non-profit organization, to influence specific legislation or government policy. Lobbyists possess specialized knowledge of the legislative process and maintain relationships with policymakers to represent and advance their clients' interests. Unlike general advocates, lobbyists must register with government bodies and disclose their activities and finances to ensure transparency.

Key Differences

- **Purpose and Motivation:** Advocates are motivated by cause-based goals and focus on broader social changes, while specific legislative or policy objectives drive lobbyists for their clients.

- **Activities:** Advocates use public campaigns and awareness strategies, while lobbyists engage directly with lawmakers and government officials to influence specific legislation or regulations.
- **Regulation and Transparency:** Lobbyists are subject to regulatory requirements that mandate registration and reporting, promoting transparency. Advocates, particularly those not employed by specific organizations, may not have similar obligations.

What Is Advocacy?

Advocacy is a multifaceted practice embedded in various aspects of social interaction. Key elements include:

- **Communication and Information:** Advocates effectively convey messages and data to inform, persuade, and initiate action.
- **Social and Cultural Navigation:** They use social norms and cultural values to reach people personally.
- **Sales and Relationships:** Advocates sell ideas and build relationships to promote these ideas.
- **Persuasion, Trust, and Integrity:** Advocacy relies on ethical persuasion, trust-building, and maintaining integrity.
- **Honesty, Passion, and Commitment:** These attributes are crucial for sincere and impactful advocacy.
- **Negotiation and Compromise:** Advocates often mediate between interests, negotiate terms, and foster compromise to achieve practical solutions.

What Is Lobbying?

Lobbying involves attempting to influence decisions made by government officials, primarily legislators or regulatory agencies. Lobbyists advocate for specific causes or policies to persuade officials to enact or modify legislation or policies to align with their interests. Key aspects include:

- **Communication:** Providing information, research, and expert advice to policymakers.
- **Advocacy:** Arguing for specific outcomes in public policies and laws.
- **Representation:** Representing the interests of a group or entity.
- **Monitoring:** Tracking legislative and regulatory processes that affect their interests.
- **Relationship Building:** Establishing and maintaining relationships with key decision makers.

Lobbying is regulated to ensure transparency and prevent corruption. Lobbyists must register their activities and disclose expenditures and the entities they represent. Lobbying is a fundamental part of democratic systems, enabling stakeholders to participate in politics.

Who Is a Professional Advocate?

Professional advocates must possess several essential qualities all of which are outlined below. You must have the majority of these abilities to be effective. If not, your job is going to be difficult:

1. **Relationship Builder:** Creating and maintaining robust networks with policymakers, stakeholders, and the public.

2. **Public Policy Management:** Influencing public policy through insights, data, and persuasive arguments.

3. **Political Access Provider:** Ensuring diverse voices are heard in the political arena.

4. **Accountability Expert:** Holding institutions and leaders accountable.

5. **Constitutional Knowledge:** Using a deep understanding of constitutional law to defend rights and navigate legal landscapes.

6. **Facilitator:** Organizing discussions, setting agendas, and creating platforms for dialogue.

Who Is a Professional Lobbyist?

Effective lobbyists have unique personal qualities which allow them to work directly with policy makers and regulators. These traits are the cornerstone to good negotiations:

1. **Persuasiveness:** Crafting compelling arguments and emotionally connecting with stakeholders.

2. **Strategic Thinking:** Anticipating legislative movements and adapting strategies.

3. **Integrity:** Operating with high ethical standards to build trust and credibility.

4. **Communication Skills:** Conveying complex ideas clearly and concisely.

5. **Networking Abilities:** Maintaining extensive professional networks.

6. **Negotiation Skills:** Brokering deals and resolving conflicts.

7. **Resilience:** Bouncing back from setbacks and handling high-pressure environments.

8. **Attention to Detail:** Understanding legislative nuances and personal details about lawmakers.

9. **Analytical Skills:** Analyzing legislation, political trends, and potential outcomes.

10. **Adaptability:** Shifting tactics in response to changing political climates and emerging technologies.

Advocate Milieu

The environment within which advocates operate is shaped by:

- **Legal and Regulatory Framework:** Understanding human rights, free speech, and assembly laws.
- **Political Environment:** Adapting to the political climate and building relationships accordingly.
- **Social and Cultural Context:** Tailoring approaches resonate with cultural values and social norms.
- **Economic Factors:** Framing arguments based on economic conditions.
- **Technological Influences:** Leveraging digital platforms while considering privacy and access disparities.
- **Networks and Coalitions:** Forming coalitions to amplify influence and resources.
- **Personal Attributes:** Empathy, resilience, creativity, and integrity.
- **Ethical Considerations:** Balancing aggressive strategies with honesty, transparency, and respect.

Lobbyist Milieu

The lobbyist's environment involves:

1. **Legislative and Political Environments:** Engaging with lawmakers and regulators.
2. **Specific Interests Focus:** Representing specific interests or objectives.
3. **Regulatory Frameworks:** Navigating legal frameworks for effective lobbying.
4. **Ethics and Transparency:** Adhering to ethical practices and transparency requirements.
5. **Professional Networks:** Maintaining extensive government and industry connections.
6. **Negotiation Skills:** Brokering mutually acceptable solutions.
7. **Tactical Adaptability:** Adapting strategies to dynamic political and legislative conditions.

What an Advocate Isn't

Advocates are not lobbyists or traditional influencers. While they may engage in policy discussions, their primary allegiance is to the truth and the public interest, not private clients. They are informed spokespersons driven by knowledge and ethical standards.

What a Lobbyist Isn't

A lobbyist isn't a politician, lawmaker, or government official who directly creates or enacts legislation. They are also not simply a protester or activist, as their role involves more structured, behind-the-scenes engagement with legislators rather than public demonstrations or campaigns. Lobbyists are not just corporate spokespeople nor are they merely persuasive salespeople trying to push personal opinions or sell products. They do not have the power to vote on laws or make final decisions on policy but instead work to influence those who do by presenting research, information, and arguments to shape legislative outcomes on behalf of their clients or interest groups.

What Permits Us to Advocate or Lobby?

The right to advocate is a democratic principle supported by legal protections like freedom of speech and assembly and the right to petition the government. These frameworks ensure advocates can speak out without fear of undue reprisal.

Your Choice

So, what will you become? I chose the role of a professional lobbyist. It fits my moral directive of helping different groups, associations, and businesses to intervene directly in public policy development that directly affects their purpose and mission.

Understanding the roles of advocates and lobbyists reveals the mechanisms driving political, social, and economic change. By demystifying these roles, we better appreciate their essential contributions to a healthy democracy. Political involvement requires knowledge, ethics, and a commitment to the public good.

As you continue traveling through this political roadmap, prepare to be amazed by the power and impact of individual political involvement in our free society, America.

This chapter includes some valuable insights into the tools and strategies that can shape the outcome of legislative efforts. The real art of lobbying, however, lies in how these elements come together in practice. In the next chapter, we step behind the curtain and dive deep into professional lobbying, exploring real-life case studies, personal stories, and expert strategies. Get ready for an insider's guide that will inspire and equip you to master the intricate dance of influence and advocacy. The best is yet to come!

"A politician is a fellow who will lay down your life
for his country."

– Texas Guinan

Chapter 3: Understanding Your Legislative Arena

"The framers of the Constitution carefully divided power between the federal and state governments, recognizing that while the national government should address issues of broad, national concern, states and local governments are better equipped to handle the diverse needs of their communities. Each level of government has its own responsibilities, but all three must work together to serve the people effectively."

—Sandra Day O'Connor

O ver the years, my experience working with the three levels of government—local, state, and federal—has taught me invaluable lessons about the distinct characteristics of each and the unique approaches required to navigate them effectively. Each election brings change: new faces, new priorities, and new dynamics, which require constant adaptation. Whether dealing with local city council members focused on community-specific issues, state legislators balancing regional concerns, or federal representatives handling national policies, I learned that understanding their backgrounds, personalities, and motivations was critical. No two elected officials approach their work the same way, and trial by error taught me how to tailor my style and strategies to fit the needs of each arena. Some efforts succeeded spectacularly, while others fell flat, but every experience sharpened my skills and deepened my understanding of how to work within these systems.

Lobbying at each level is as much about adjusting to the people as it is about understanding the process. Local government often demands grassroots, community-oriented approach, while state lobbying requires building coalitions and mastering regional political dynamics. At the federal level, advocacy takes on a more specialized and strategic tone, requiring expertise and collaboration with diverse stakeholders. I quickly realized that the strategies that worked in one arena wouldn't necessarily succeed in another, and I had to remain flexible, creative, and open to change. While navigating the many personalities and backgrounds of legislators wasn't always easy, it taught me how to listen, adapt, and seize opportunities when they arose. Each experience, whether a success or a misstep, contributed to my growth as both a lobbyist and an advocate, shaping my ability to respond to the ever-changing landscape of government.

In this chapter you will learn

- About the three different levels of government.
- What makes each level distinct.
- The unique styles of lobbying tailored to each arena.

Welcome to the wild world of American democracy, where government operates like a three-ring circus at local, state, and federal levels. Each ringmaster (or government level) has its own responsibilities and powers designed to address specific needs. Equally important are the performers—lobbyists and advocates—who aim to influence decisions across these levels. This chapter takes you through each level's structure and functions and reveals the unique lobbying strategies necessary to navigate them effectively. Buckle up, it's showtime!

Local Government

Municipal Government: Municipal governments, often called city or town councils, handle local affairs that directly affect one's daily life. These people manage your potholes, public safety, and local parks. They're also the ones you can bump into at the grocery store, making lobbying here a more direct (and sometimes awkwardly personal) affair. If you play your cards right, you could end up chatting policy over a gallon of milk.

County Government: County governments operate above the municipal level and cover broader areas, including multiple towns or cities. Imagine your local government but with a bigger budget and a bit more swagger. They manage things like public health facilities, regional roads, and the local jail. Lobbying at this level often requires a broader approach, targeting regional development and public works. Think of it as leveling up in the game of local politics.

Special Districts: Special districts are like the superheroes of local government. Their powers are concentrated and focused with specific missions such as managing schools or water supplies. They fly under the radar. Lobbying here involves dealing with stakeholders who are directly impacted by the district's policies, like parents in school districts or farmers in irrigation districts. It's all about hitting the right nerve.

Lobbying at the local level is the grassroots campaign trail. It's more personal and direct, often involving town hall meetings, local committees, or one-on-one chats with elected officials. The scale is smaller, but the impact can be immediate and significant. Plus, you might get invited to the town's annual BBQ—if you play your cards right.

State Government

The Legislative Branch: The state legislative branch, typically a bicameral system with a house of representatives and a senate is where state laws are crafted. (Nebraska likes to be the odd one with its unicameral setup.) Legislators represent local districts, making them prime targets for lobbying by constituents and interest groups. Picture a political chess game where every move counts, and the stakes are your state's future.

The Executive Branch: Led by the governor, the state executive branch is like the CEO of State, Inc. It implements laws and oversees the state government's functions. This branch includes other key players like the lieutenant governor and attorney general. Lobbying here involves influencing regulatory practices and the enforcement of laws. It's less about the sizzle and more about the steak.

The Judicial Branch: The state's judicial branch interprets state laws and administers justice. It includes everything from lower courts to the state supreme court. While direct lobbying is forbidden, broader advocacy can focus on judicial reform or issues affecting the court's decision-making environment. Think of it as lobbying the refs rather than the players.

Lobbying at the state level is more complex than lobbying at the local level. It involves activities from testifying at legislative hearings to statewide advocacy campaigns. Lobbyists here may represent professional associations, corporations, or non-profits seeking to influence legislation or state policy. It's like moving from high school sports to college Division 1—everything's bigger, faster, and more competitive.

Federal Government

Congress: The U.S. Congress, divided into the House of Representatives and the Senate, is the heavyweight champion of legislative power. It enacts laws, declares war, and approves federal spending. Lobbyists swarm this arena like bees to honey, representing every sector from tech giants to environmental groups. If you can make it here, you can make it anywhere.

President: The President isn't just the head honcho of the executive branch; they're the policy trendsetter. Presidential decisions have vast implications, making this office a prime focus for lobbyists aiming to influence executive orders and federal policies. It's like trying to whisper in the ear of the most powerful person in the world while they're on stage at a rock concert.

Federal Courts: The federal judiciary, including the Supreme Court, influences the country's broad legal principles. While direct lobbying is a no-no here, broader advocacy efforts can shape public opinion and legislative action that indirectly affect judicial decisions. It's a high-stakes game of 3D chess, with moves that resonate through the ages.

Lobbying at the federal level is the big leagues. It involves sophisticated strategies, coalition building, direct lobbying, and public campaigns. The stakes are high, and the strategy is elaborate, often requiring significant resources and coordination. It's like the Super Bowl of politics, where only the best-prepared teams have a shot at victory.

Lobbying styles vary by government level, reflecting their distinct scopes and powers. Local lobbying is straightforward, focusing on immediate community concerns. State lobbying combines direct action with broader strategic campaigns to influence state-wide policies. At the federal level, lobbying is a high-stakes, resource-intensive endeavor, often requiring coalitions of diverse stakeholders to make a significant impact.

I chose the state government and regulatory agencies as my arena of operations. I found that my influence had a broader reach, and I could have an immediate effect for my clients. Decisions happen more quickly with immediate outcomes. It is fast paced and keeps you on your toes. Rewards or heartbreak are immediate.

This chapter demystifies the operations of each governmental level and the corresponding lobbying approaches necessary to influence them effectively. Whether you're working the local beat or swinging for the fences at the federal level, understanding the unique dynamics of each arena is key to your success. So, get ready to dive in—no swan dives required—and make some waves in the political pool!

> "Giving money and power to government is like giving whiskey and car keys to teenage boys."
>
> — P. J. O'Rourke

Chapter 4: **Sign Here Please**

"The pen is mightier than the sword, especially when
it signs you up to change the world."

—Unknown

I still remember the excitement of registering for the first time with the secretary of state and officially becoming a lobbyist. Completing the registration process felt like a milestone—one that came with both pride and a sense of responsibility. I could finally call myself a lobbyist, joining a profession I deeply respected. At the time, I was focused on the opportunities ahead: working with legislators, advocating for causes, and navigating the intricacies of the legislative process. What I didn't fully appreciate, however, was the level of detail and diligence required to stay on top of the reporting obligations that came with the title. Every activity, every dollar spent, and every client engagement had to be meticulously documented and reported within strict timeframes.

Early in my career, I made the mistake of becoming complacent with my reporting, and it cost me dearly. For four months, I failed to file my reports on time, thinking I could just catch up later. That mistake resulted in an $800 fine—an expensive and humbling lesson. It taught me that being a lobbyist isn't just about relationships and advocacy; it's about maintaining professionalism and adhering to the rules that keep the process transparent and accountable. From that point forward, I made it a personal rule to file my reports on time, no matter how busy I was. If there's one piece of advice I would pass on to any new lobbyist, it's this: never underestimate the importance of the details. The deadlines matter, and learning that lesson the hard way is not worth the cost.

In this chapter you will learn

- Why you must register.
- How you register.
- How to declare your status: volunteer or professional lobbyist.
- What you can do as a professional lobbyist.
- What you can't do as a professional lobbyist.
- Your reporting requirements.
- The lobbying rules for the House and Senate.

Understanding the intricacies of the lobbying process is crucial. This chapter will provide a detailed explanation of each category, offering comprehensive insights into the lobbying process. This understanding will help you appreciate the importance of the registration process and keep you legal and out of trouble with regulators.

Why You Must Register

Registration in lobbying is not a mere bureaucratic formality. It's a foundational step to legitimize your influence in the legislative process. It's your license to operate. Each state has its rules, but the essence remains the same: transparency, accountability, and public trust. By registering, you make your activities visible to the public and lawmakers, ensuring everyone knows who is behind the curtain pulling the levers of persuasion.

Why is registration crucial? Lobbying can sway significant legislative decisions, affecting thousands. Without a transparent system, undisclosed influences could undermine democratic processes. Registration helps to mitigate these risks by providing a clear trail of who is lobbying whom, for what purpose, and with what financial backing.

Moreover, registration acts as a gatekeeper, ensuring that only those who are serious and ethical about their lobbying gain entrance. It sets the stage for responsible conduct in the lobbying arena. By complying, you signal your commitment to playing by the rules, maintaining integrity in your professional conduct, and upholding the values of the democratic process.

> **Pro Tip:** Check your state's lobbying requirements to ensure you are legal before lobbying (ttps://www.ncsl.org/ethics/lobbyist-registration-requirements).

How You Register

Registering as a lobbyist is akin to preparing for a major expedition. First, you must understand the landscape. This means familiarizing yourself with the state's specific requirements where you intend to lobby. Generally, this involves visiting the secretary of state's website and navigating to the lobbying section. Here, you will find registration forms requiring comprehensive details about your identity, your clients, the legislative or regulatory interests you advocate for, and other pertinent information.

The process doesn't stop at filling out forms; it extends to understanding the periodic updates and reaffirmations required to keep your registration current. Depending on the state, registration fees may be involved and failing to pay these can result in losing your lobbying privileges.

Digital tools have simplified this process significantly. Most states now offer online registration systems that guide you step by step, ensuring you meet all legal requirements. These systems also provide resources and support to help navigate the complexities of lobbying laws, making the registration process as streamlined as possible while ensuring compliance with all regulatory demands.

> **Pro Tip:** Check your regulatory agency's home page. There, you will find a link to sign up as a lobbyist.

Declaring Your Status

When you register, you must declare is whether you are a volunteer or a professional lobbyist. This distinction is crucial because it sets the expectations for your activities and regulatory oversight.

Volunteer lobbyists typically engage in lobbying activities on an unpaid basis, often for causes they are passionate about, such as community issues, non-profit advocacy, or specific civic engagements. Despite not being compensated, volunteer lobbyists are still subject to many of the same reporting and ethical standards as professional lobbyists.

On the other hand, professional lobbyists are compensated for their efforts and often represent businesses, trade associations, or other business entities. As a professional, the expectations are higher, and so is the scrutiny. You are usually seen as having more at stake, more resources at your disposal, and potentially more influence, which comes with a greater responsibility to maintain transparency and integrity in your dealings.

What You Can Do as a Professional Lobbyist

As a professional lobbyist, your primary role is to advocate for your clients' interests. This involves various activities, from direct lobbying, which includes meeting with and persuading legislators and their staff to indirect lobbying, such as organizing grassroots campaigns to mobilize public opinion. You are the bridge between private interests and public policy; your negotiation, public speaking, and strategic planning skills are vital.

In addition to advocacy, professional lobbyists often monitor and report legislative developments that could affect their clients. This involves staying informed about legislative sessions, committee hearings, and any changes in the political landscape. By providing expert analysis and timely information, you help clients understand potential impacts and strategize accordingly.

> **Pro Tip:** Check your regulatory agency for the legislative citation link that explains what you can and cannot do as a lobbyist in your state.

What You Can't Do as a Professional Lobbyist

The role of a lobbyist comes with boundaries that are strictly enforced by law. Prohibited activities include, but are not limited to, offering gifts of significant value to influence a legislator's decision, engaging in lobbying activities without proper registration, or misrepresenting information to public officials. These restrictions prevent corruption and ensure lobbying is conducted ethically and transparently.

Furthermore, lobbyists are restricted from promising political support in exchange for favorable votes or threatening political consequences for the opposition. Such practices could undermine the integrity of the decision-making process and lead to public distrust in the legislative system.

Reporting Requirements

Transparency is not a one-time requirement at the point of registration. You must report on an ongoing basis on your lobbying activities, financial expenditures, and the interests you represent. This includes detailed accounts of meetings with lawmakers, legislation you are working on, expenses incurred during lobbying efforts, and any contributions made to political campaigns.

These reports must be filed regularly—monthly, quarterly, or annually—and made accessible to the public. This ongoing disclosure serves as a continuous check on your activities, ensuring you remain accountable to your clients and the public. It helps maintain transparency that supports the democratic process by informing the public about who influences legislation and policy.

> *Pro Tip:* You do not want to miss your filing date. Make sure you add all reporting due dates to your calendar. You can be fined for missing reports, and the fines can be substantial. I missed several dates and was fined $800.00. After that mistake, I never missed another reporting date.

> *Pro Tip:* Lobbying Rules for the House and Senate

Each legislative body operates with its rules and norms regarding lobbying. The rules for the House and Senate can differ significantly regarding access to legislators, the types of communication allowed, and specific restrictions during sessions.

For instance, the senate may have strict rules about lobbying on the Senate floor or during committee meetings. In contrast, the House might have more lenient regulations regarding interactions in certain areas. Understanding these nuances is crucial for effective advocacy. You must be aware of and respect these boundaries to maintain good relations and credibility with legislators.

Additionally, both bodies often have rules regarding electronic communications, such as emails and social media interactions with legislators. Staying abreast of these guidelines and adapting your strategies accordingly is essential for compliance and effective lobbying.

By fully grasping and respecting the rules of engagement in each legislative body you ensure that your advocacy efforts are effective and compliant with the established norms and legal requirements.

You have registered, are legal, and are now part of the process. The next chapter will cover how to identify the issues you want to get involved with and the ones you don't. You decide the issues you feel comfortable with, issues you can champion.

"Politics is the only field where you get to campaign
on fixing problems you created."

— Unknown

Chapter 5: Choosing the Right Fights

"A successful lobbyist knows that you can't fight every battle. You need to carefully choose the issues that align with your strengths, the interests of your client, and the political environment. Picking the right issue means focusing on where you can make the most impact and where success is achievable."

—*Larry O'Brien*

Over the years, I've learned that the best way to find new clients and support their issues is through networking, visibility, and being proactive. Some of my most valuable client relationships started in unexpected ways, simply because I made myself present and engaged in the right settings. For example, Ford Motor Company became a client after we happened to be golfing partners at a Chamber of Commerce tournament. CNA Insurance reached out to me after hearing me speak at an agent's meeting, recognizing my understanding of their industry's needs. Similarly, the Independent Electrical Contractors of Colorado hired me after their executive director attended my presentation at the Colorado Society of Association Executives' Day at the Capitol. These opportunities didn't just happen by chance—they were the result of showing up, building credibility, and demonstrating my ability to provide value.

Being proactive has always been at the core of how I build relationships and tackle issues. I don't sit back and wait for opportunities to find me—I seek them out, identify where I can make a difference, and connect with the right people. I've worked hard to know the issues I can handle and, just as importantly, to recognize the ones I can't. This clarity has allowed me to focus on areas where I can be most effective and deliver real results. Whether it's through a speech, a casual conversation on the golf course, or a professional meeting, I've made it a point to stay visible, engaged, and ready to act. That commitment has been key to building strong relationships and achieving success for my clients.

In this chapter you will learn

- How to identify the right issues to lobby for.
- The importance of aligning with your values and goals.
- Strategies for researching and selecting issues.
- Tips on staying focused and avoiding advocacy burnout.

Welcome to the thrill of choosing your issues in lobbying. We live in turbulent times, and new problems appear every day. Think of it as a strategic game of Whac-A-Mole, where you pick which mole to whack with your oversized mallet of justice. It's not just about swinging aimlessly; it's about precision, timing, and knowing which mole is worth your energy and what you want to be associated with. This chapter will guide you through identifying the issues to advocate for, aligning them with your values and goals, and ensuring you're swinging that mallet with purpose and panache.

Aligning Lobbying with Your Values and Goals

Before diving into the sea of issues, it's crucial to understand your values and goals clearly. It's like choosing a flavor of ice cream: Do you go for classic vanilla or something wild like bubble gum? Knowing what you stand for will help you decide which causes are worth your time and effort. This is a comprehensive list. I don't use all of them when deciding what I want to support and get involved in. I use those that work on the issue I am trying to settle. Use what works for you.

1. **Self-Reflection:** Take a moment (or a few) to ponder what matters most to you. Is it environmental protection, social justice, health care, or something else entirely? Grab a cup of coffee, sit in your favorite thinking spot, and let your mind wander. Write down your thoughts—sometimes, seeing them in black and white can provide clarity.

Exercise: Grab a notebook and jot down answers to the following questions:

- *What are the top three issues that make your blood boil?*
- *If you could change one thing in your community, what would it be?*
- *What stories or news topics consistently grab your attention?*
- *What political and economic issues are affecting public policy?*

---

2. **Long-Term Goals:** Consider where you see yourself in the next five, ten, or twenty years. What kind of impact do you want to have? Do you want to be the person who helped save the charitable gaming industry (Bingo) or the one who fought for a more vibrant business environment? Identifying and setting long-term goals will help you stay focused and motivated.

Exercise: Write a mission statement for your advocacy journey. It should be a short, inspiring sentence that encapsulates your vision for the future.

---

3. **Passion Check:** Be passionate about your chosen issues. Passion is the fuel that keeps the advocacy engine running, especially when the road gets bumpy. If the thought of the issue makes you want to jump out of bed in the morning (or at least not hit snooze for the tenth time), you're on the right track.

> *Pro Tip:* Try volunteering or attending events related to the issues you're passionate about. This will give you a better sense of your commitment and help you connect with like-minded individuals.

Researching and Selecting Issues

Now that you've sorted your values and goals, it's time to dive into the nitty-gritty of researching and selecting the correct issues. Consider yourself a detective. Magnifying glass in hand, get ready to uncover the most pressing and impactful causes.

> *Pro Tip:* Understanding the issues will allow you to identify prospective clients you can approach for legislative representation and expand your client base.

1. **Current Events:** Stay updated on current events. Read newspapers, watch the news, follow reputable sources on social media, and maybe even engage in a little light eavesdropping at the local coffee shop. The world is constantly changing, and staying informed will help you spot emerging issues that need attention.

Pro Tip: Create news alerts for keywords related to your areas of interest. This will ensure you receive updates on relevant developments.

2. **Community Needs:** Look around your community. What issues are people talking about? What problems are they facing? Sometimes the most impactful advocacy starts right in your backyard. Attend town hall meetings, join community groups, or converse with neighbors.

Pro Tip: Conduct a survey or host a focus group to gather your community's input on the most pressing issues. Your chamber of commerce can be a wealth of information on community issues.

3. **Data and Reports:** Dive into research reports, data sets, and studies related to potential issues. Numbers don't lie (unless they're on your bathroom scale). Analyzing data can help you understand the scope and impact of various problems, allowing you to prioritize effectively.

Pro Tip: Websites like Pew Research Center, government databases, and academic journals are treasure troves of information.

4. **Expert Opinions:** Talk to experts and stakeholders in various fields. They can provide insights and perspectives that you might not have considered. Plus, it's always good to sound smart at parties.

Pro Tip: Contact a local university or research institution to find experts willing to share their knowledge. Attend webinars, workshops, or seminars on topics of interest. Get involved with political parties. They have their fingers on the pulse of political issues.

5. **SWOT Analysis:** Conduct a SWOT (Strengths, Weaknesses, Opportunities, Threats) analysis for each potential issue. This will help you evaluate the feasibility and impact of your advocacy efforts.

> *Pro Tip:* Create a table with four quadrants (Strengths, Weaknesses, Opportunities, and Threats) and list relevant points for each issue you are considering.

Staying Focused and Avoiding Burnout

Choosing your battles is only half the game. Staying focused and avoiding lobbing burnout is equally essential. After all, you can't fight every battle and certainly can't fight them all at once.

1. **Set Realistic Goals:** Break down your advocacy efforts into manageable goals. Rome wasn't built in a day, nor will your advocacy empire. Small, achievable goals will keep you motivated and prevent feeling overwhelmed.

> *Pro Tip:* Set your goals using the SMART criteria (Specific, Measurable, Achievable, Relevant, and Time-bound). We all know this technique. Use it to your advantage.

2. **Prioritize:** Learn to prioritize issues based on urgency and impact. Use the Eisenhower matrix or a good pros-and-cons list to determine what needs your attention first. Remember, it's okay to let some moles stay un-whacked.

Pro Tip: Create a priority matrix with four quadrants: (1) Urgent and Important, (2) Not Urgent but Important, (3) Urgent but Not Important, and (4) Not Urgent and Not Important. This method always brings clarity to the issue.

3. **Delegate and Collaborate:** Don't hesitate to delegate tasks and collaborate. Lobbying is a team sport, not a solo mission. Build a network of like-minded individuals and organizations to share the load and amplify your impact.

Pro Tip: List potential partners and collaborators. Reach out to them and explore opportunities for joint efforts.

4. **Self-Care:** Take care of yourself. Lobbing can be exhausting, and burnout is real. Make time for hobbies, relaxation, and, most important, laughter. Watch a funny movie, read a humorous book, or laugh with friends. Remember, a happy lobbyist is an effective advocate.

Pro Tip: Schedule regular breaks and downtime in your calendar to ensure you have time to recharge. Take care of yourself so you can take care of your clients.

5. **Celebrate Small Wins:** Don't wait for the big victory to celebrate. Acknowledge and celebrate the small wins along the way. This will keep your spirits high and remind you that progress is being made.

Pro Tip: Keep a journal of your achievements, no matter how small. Reflecting on your progress can be a great morale booster. Seeing things in writing gives you concrete evidence that you are moving forward toward your legislative goals.

Advanced Strategies for Effective Lobbying

Once you have identified your issues, clients, and goals, it's time to employ advanced strategies to enhance your lobbying efforts. These strategies will help maximize your impact and ensure your voice is heard.

1. **Storytelling:** People connect with stories more than statistics. Craft compelling narratives highlighting the human element of the issues you care about. Share personal stories, anecdotes, and case studies to make your cause relatable and impactful.

Pro Tip: Write a short narrative about your cause, focusing on the personal impact and emotional appeal. Share it with friends or colleagues for feedback.

2. **Use of Media:** Leverage traditional and social media to amplify your message. Write op-eds, create blog posts, and engage with social media platforms to reach a broader audience. Visual content like infographics and videos can also be powerful tools.

Pro Tip: Develop a media strategy that includes a content calendar, key messages, and target platforms. Create a media calendar that schedules your messages to the audience you are trying to influence.

3. **Lobbying and Advocacy Campaigns:** Engage in lobbying efforts by meeting with policymakers, attending public hearings, and participating in advocacy campaigns. Building

relationships with decision-makers can significantly influence policy outcomes and clients.

Exercise: Research your local representatives and schedule meetings to discuss your issues. Prepare a concise and persuasive pitch for your cause.

---

4. **Grassroots Mobilization:** Mobilize supporters at the grassroots level by organizing rallies, petitions, and community events to build momentum and demonstrate widespread support for your cause.

> *Pro Tip:* Use online tools like Change.org or other social media platforms to gather signatures and support for petitions.

5. **Coalition Building:** Form coalitions with other organizations and individuals who share your goals. A united front can be more effective in influencing change than working alone.

> *Pro Tip:* Identify potential coalition partners and reach out to discuss mutual goals and collaboration opportunities.

6. **Policy Analysis and Proposal:** Conduct thorough policy analysis to understand the nuances of the issues and develop well-researched proposals for change. Presenting solid evidence and clear solutions can make your lobbying more persuasive and educates legislators on your issue.

> *Pro Tip:* Utilize think tanks, academic institutions, and policy research organizations for data and analysis. Search online to find resources that supports your position.

7. **Monitoring and Evaluation:** Continuously monitor and evaluate your advocacy efforts. Track progress, measure outcomes, and adjust your strategies to improve effectiveness.

> *Pro Tip:* Develop a monitoring and evaluation plan with specific indicators to measure the success of your advocacy activities.

Choosing the correct issues to advocate for is like navigating a maze with hidden treasures. You never know what is around every corner. By aligning your advocacy with your values and goals, staying informed, and maintaining a healthy balance, you can make a meaningful impact without losing your sanity. So, grab your mallet, aim carefully, and start whacking those metaphorical moles of injustice.

Remember, lobbying is not a sprint but a marathon. Stay committed, be adaptable, and celebrate each step forward, no matter how small. You can create lasting change and make a difference with passion, persistence, and the right strategies.

I have found my issues and clients in many ways. One of the individuals in my foursome in a golf tournament sponsored by my local chamber of commerce was a Ford Motor executive. During our play, we talked about issues affecting the automotive industry in Colorado. The executive was having trouble connecting with legislators. After we finished our play, the executive asked me to come by his office later. We discussed his problem in detail, resulting in the Ford Motor Company becoming a client. You never know when or where you will discover an issue and a new client.

"Democracy is the art and science of running the circus from the monkey cage."

— H. L. Mencken

Chapter 6: The Secret Sauce to Finding the Perfect Client

"The perfect client is one whose goals align with your values, knowledge, and strategic expertise. A good lobbyist doesn't just take on any client; they choose those whose issues they are passionate about and where they can add the most value. Success comes when you believe in your client's mission and can use your skills to drive their objectives forward."

—Paul A. Miller

Navigating the nuanced and influential lobbying world requires more than just knowledge of the legislative process; it necessitates a profound understanding of relationship dynamics. A successful lobbyist must identify, cultivate, and sometimes terminate client relationships with precision and ethics. This comprehensive guide explores who the perfect client is and practical strategies to find them, how to handle different types of clients like volunteers and business professionals, and how to end client engagements when they no longer serve a mutual benefit.

In this chapter you will learn about

- Characteristics of the perfect client.
- Strategies for finding the perfect client.
- Differences in working with volunteers versus business professionals.
- Signs a client relationship is ending and procedures for terminating such a relationship.
- Handling different client scenarios.
- Building long-term client relationships.
- Crafting a diverse client portfolio.
- Leveraging technology in client management.
- Adapting to changes in the lobbying landscape.

Who Is the Perfect Client?

In the complex lobbying arena, a perfect client is akin to a strategic partner who shares your commitment to ethics, effectiveness, and clear communication. Such clients are leaders in their respective fields and share a robust commitment to engaging in the public policy process transparently and responsibly.

Characteristics of the Perfect Client

- **Informed:** They thoroughly understand their industry's landscape and regulatory challenges, enabling them to provide clear and precise communication of their needs and goals.
- **Engaged:** Their involvement goes beyond passive observation; they actively participate in crafting strategies and are responsive to changes in the legislative environment.

- **Ethical:** They adhere to the highest standards of integrity, ensuring that all lobbying activities are conducted within legal frameworks and ethical guidelines.
- **Realistic:** They set achievable goals and maintain practical expectations about lobbying efforts' timelines and success rates.
- **Communicative:** Effective communication is key to any successful relationship; the perfect client provides feedback, is open to discussions, and is transparent.
- **Well-Funded:** The perfect client has the financial resources to conduct a legislative campaign.

Finding the Perfect Client

Finding the perfect client involves strategic networking, reputation building, and targeted outreach. I have found clients by being involved in my local chamber of commerce, rotary club, college alumni association meetings, and my professional association. You just never know when you will run into someone who needs your expertise and service.

Networking

Active engagement in industry events, legislative hearings, and networking groups is crucial. These platforms allow lobbyists to display their expertise, listen to and learn about a potential client's needs and objectives and showcase their skills while evaluating if they are a mutual fit. Picture it as speed dating, but for policy works. You get to showcase your skills while assessing whether there's a professional fit.

Content Marketing

Publishing insightful articles, engaging in public speaking, and maintaining a robust social media presence establishes a lobbyist as a thought leader in their field. This strategy enhances visibility and attracts clients who value knowledgeable and proactive representation. Think of it as creating a magnetic force field that pulls in the right kind of attention.

Client Referrals

Utilizing a network of satisfied clients can be the most direct pathway to new business. Clients who have had positive experiences are often willing to refer others, providing an introduction that comes with built-in trust. It's like having your group of cheerleaders who also happen to wield influence.

Targeted Outreach

Understanding market needs through research enables you to approach potential clients most likely to benefit from your services. Customized pitches highlighting past successes and specific expertise related to the client's industry can be particularly effective. Imagine crafting a personalized love letter to each potential client, but instead of flowers, you're offering strategic victories for their political interests.

> **Pro Tip:** My elevator speech is short and sweet. It is simply, "I am the guy you hire to protect you from the people you elect." It stops them in their tracks and gets them to want to know how you can help them. That's when meaningful dialog occurs between you and your prospective client.

Working with Volunteers vs. Businesspeople

Lobbying for volunteer-driven organizations versus for-profit business entities presents distinct challenges and requires tailored approaches for each.

Volunteers

- **Passion vs. Professionalism:** Volunteers often bring passion and dedication to their causes. However, they lack professional lobbying experience or understanding, necessitating more comprehensive guidance and education from the lobbyist. Think of them as enthusiastic puppies needing training to channel their energy effectively.

- **Resource Constraints:** Typically operating with fewer resources, volunteer organizations may rely heavily on the lobbyist's ability to mobilize support and resources effectively. It's like making a gourmet meal with a shoestring budget. You must be creative and resourceful.

Businesspeople

- **Result Oriented:** Business clients are often more focused on outcomes that can directly influence their company's bottom line. They tend to be results oriented and may have higher expectations for quick, effective advocacy. It's like working with someone who wants to see the money rolling in yesterday.

- **Resource Availability:** Unlike volunteer groups, business clients usually have more resources, which can be leveraged to support more extensive lobbying campaigns. This is like having a well-stocked kitchen—everything you need is at your fingertips to create a feast.

Navigating these dynamics involves understanding each type of client's inherent motivations and constraints, adapting communication strategies, and setting clear, mutually agreed-upon goals.

> **Pro Tip:** Ask yourself: what clients did I enjoy working with? What clients didn't I enjoy working with? What did I learn from those experiences?

Firing the Client

Terminating a client relationship is significant and fraught with potential complications. However, it can sometimes be necessary to maintain professional integrity and personal sanity.

Signs a Termination Might Be Necessary

- **Misalignment of Goals:** Persistent differences in desired outcomes or strategies that cannot be reconciled.
- **Ethical Concerns:** Disagreements over ethical approaches to lobbying that could jeopardize professional standards.
- **Lack of Progress:** Continuous lack of progress can lead to frustration on both sides, indicating that a change is needed.

Procedure for Termination

- **Assessment:** Regular reviews of client relationships can help identify issues before they become critical.
- **Communication:** Open discussions about concerns might resolve misunderstandings. If not, they set the stage for a respectful termination.

- **Documentation:** Keeping thorough records of all interactions and attempts at resolution can support the decision to part ways if necessary.

Handling Different Client Scenarios

The Overzealous Volunteer Group

Working with volunteer groups can be both rewarding and challenging. These clients are usually passionate but may need a more professional understanding of the legislative process. The more training you can giver to your volunteers, the more comfortable they will be with the process and their role in that process. You must manage their expectations and guide their energy to be effective. These steps will help you accomplish your goals.

- **Education Sessions:** Conduct workshops or training sessions to educate volunteers on the legislative process and realistic timelines for achieving goals. The better trained the better your chances of success.
- **Clear Communication:** Set clear expectations regarding what can be achieved and the resources required.
- **Motivational Support:** Help them channel their passion into productive activities like grassroots campaigns, social media advocacy, and community outreach. Recognizing individual achievements.

The Demanding Business Professional

Business clients are typically results driven and may have high expectations for quick outcomes. To manage these relationships effectively, you should do the following:

- **Detailed Planning:** Present a detailed plan with timelines, milestones, and clear deliverables. This can help set realistic expectations and provide a roadmap for success.
- **Regular Updates:** Provide regular updates and progress reports to keep the client informed. Transparency builds trust and keeps them engaged in the process.
- **Outcome-Focused Communication:** Emphasize how the lobbying efforts will translate into tangible benefits for their business. Connect the dots between advocacy activities and potential business outcomes.

Building Long-Term Client Relationships

Successful lobbying is not just about achieving immediate goals but also about building long-term relationships with clients. Here are some ideas for cultivating and maintaining these relationships:

- **Continuous Engagement:** Stay in touch with clients even during off-seasons. Regular check-ins, holiday greetings, and updates on relevant legislative changes can keep the relationship warm.
- **Value Addition:** Always look for ways to add value beyond the immediate lobbying efforts. This could be through industry insights, hosting networking events, or offering strategic advice on related matters.
- **Feedback Loop:** Create a feedback loop where clients can provide input on the services they receive. This helps continuously improve the service and shows clients that their opinions are valued.

Crafting a Client Portfolio

Having a diverse client portfolio can enhance a lobbyist's credibility and stability. Here are some actions for how to build and manage a balanced portfolio:

- **Diversification:** Work with a mix of clients from different sectors. This not only spreads risk but also broadens your knowledge base and influence.
- **Balancing Act:** Balance high-demand clients who require intensive support with those with lower demands. This helps manage the workload and maintain the quality of service.
- **Regular Review:** Review your client portfolio to ensure it aligns with your business goals and ethical standards. Be prepared to make adjustments as needed.

Leveraging Technology in Client Management

In today's digital age, leveraging technology can greatly enhance client management. Technology provides you the edge and ensures your success with your client's goal. You decide what technology to use based upon your plan. You take advantage of that technology to get your job done. You don't have to take advantage of all of it. Here are some tools and strategies:

- **CRM Systems:** Customer Relationship Management (CRM) systems can help track client interactions, manage communications, and streamline workflows.
- **Data Analytics:** Use data analytics to gain insights into client needs, track the effectiveness of lobbying efforts, and make data-driven decisions.

- **Virtual Meetings:** Embrace virtual meeting platforms for regular check-ins and updates. This can save time and resources while maintaining strong client relationships.
- **Social Media Monitoring:** Monitor social media trends and discuss your clients' interests. This can provide valuable insights and help you craft timely and relevant advocacy strategies.

Lobbying: Adapting to Change

The lobbying landscape is constantly evolving. To stay ahead, lobbyists must be adaptable and forward thinking. Here are some ways to prepare for the future:

- **Stay Informed:** Keep abreast of legislative changes, emerging trends, and technological advancements that could impact the lobbying profession.
- **Professional Development:** Invest in continuous learning through courses, seminars, and professional networks. Staying updated with best practices and new strategies is crucial.
- **Innovative Approaches:** Be open to experimenting with new approaches and tools. Whether it's using AI for data analysis or blockchain for transparent lobbying activities, innovation can provide a competitive edge.
- **Ethical Commitment:** As public scrutiny on lobbying increases, maintaining a strong ethical commitment will be essential. Transparent practices, integrity, and accountability should be at the core of all lobbying activities.

In the intricate dance of lobbying, identifying and nurturing the right client relationships is both an art and a science. It requires strategic acumen, legal expertise, and a deep commitment to ethical practices and effective communication. Whether working with passionate volunteers or focused business leaders, understanding and adapting to their specific needs can lead to successful outcomes and long-lasting impacts on public policy.

As you gain experience, each client interaction becomes an opportunity to learn and grow. By building a diverse and balanced client portfolio, leveraging technology, and staying adaptable to change, you can navigate the complexities of the political landscape and achieve your legislative goals.

Remember, in lobbying, there is no such thing as too much preparation. Your ability to anticipate challenges and plan accordingly can make the difference between success and failure. So, arm yourself with knowledge, align your resources, and step confidently into the legislative arena. Politics might not be a game, but that doesn't mean you can't play to win.

Next, we'll uncover the core of political ambition: why individuals step into the race for office, what fuels their drive, and what distinguishes effective lawmakers from ineffective ones. We'll also delve into the unspoken expectations between lobbyists and legislators, revealing how these key players collaborate to craft the laws that shape our world. Prepare to explore the motivations, relationships, and intricate workings that bring the legislative process to life.

"I'm not saying politicians are bad people. They just have a talent for making used car salesmen look honest."

— Anonymous

Chapter 7: Tell Me Again How You Got Elected?

"There are many qualities that make a great public servant, but at the heart of every candidate for office is the desire to serve the public good. People run for office because they want to make a difference, to be part of the solution, and to have a hand in shaping the future of their community, state, or country."

—John F. Kennedy, from *Profiles in Courage*

Over the years, I've come to realize that understanding why people run for office and what they hope to accomplish is as much about reading their motivations as it is about listening to their words. Each legislator brings a unique perspective, shaped by their personal values, ambitions, and experiences, and part of my job was to figure out what made them tick. Some run for genuine reasons—they want to make a difference, fix a problem, or serve their communities—while others seem to be in it for the power, the spotlight, or to settle scores. It became a daily effort to read each legislator and understand their motivations. The good ones were confident enough to engage with me as a professional, viewing me as a resource to help them navigate complex issues. They recognized the value I brought to the table and weren't afraid of collaboration. The bad ones, on the other hand, often wore a mask of respectability, but their actions revealed something entirely different—self-interest, pettiness, or a refusal to engage honestly.

I've seen both extremes in my career. Some legislators have thanked me for my hard work, even acknowledging how my efforts helped them better understand an issue or craft a solution. Moments like that made the tough days worthwhile. But I've also dealt with legislators who saw me as a threat rather than an ally. I've had bad legislators go so far as to tell my clients they should fire me and find a new lobbyist, simply because I challenged them or didn't give them what they wanted. Those experiences were frustrating, but they also taught me to never take it personally. At the end of the day, my role has always been to advocate for my clients with integrity, professionalism, and persistence—whether I'm dealing with the best or the worst the legislature has to offer.

In this chapter you will learn

- Why people run for office.
- What makes them tick.
- What legislators expect from lobbyists.
- What lobbyists expect from legislators.
- How to work with a legislator effectively.
- What makes an effective legislator.
- What makes an ineffective legislator.

In this chapter, we explore the motivations behind the decision to run for public office. We explore the intricate interplay between personal ambition, civic duty, and political maneuvering. This chapter is a comprehensive guide to understanding the expectations and realities of life as a legislator, the symbiotic relationship with lobbyists, and the inner workings of political decision-making.

Section 1: The Call to Serve – Why Run for Office?

The desire to run for elected office is often a complex blend of personal ambition and a drive to make a difference or an event that had an effect on their personal beliefs. Many candidates are propelled by the belief that they can bring about positive change, tackling pressing issues like education reform, healthcare, and economic development. For others, it may be a career progression, a step from activism or other roles in public service to a position where they can directly influence policy. The motivations are as diverse as the individuals themselves.

> **Pro Tip:** Research the legislators you work with to identify their core motivations. Learn everything you can about them. This will make your job much easier, and you will work with them more effectively. You also will pick up various traits of each legislator as you work with them. Understanding their "why" can help sustain your commitment to working with them through challenging times.

Section 2: Expectations of a New Legislator

Upon entering office, legislators often confront a steep learning curve. They are expected to navigate complex legislative processes, represent their constituents' interests, and fulfill campaign promises. The reality of legislating can be less glamorous than anticipated, filled with bureaucratic challenges and the need for strategic compromise.

> **Pro Tip:** New legislators do not have a clue what they have gotten themselves into. It is your job to help them navigate the political environment. You know the lay of the land, and you can help them avoid the land mines every new legislator may encounter as they learn their job.

Section 3: The Psyche of a Politician – What Makes Them Tick

Understanding what drives a legislator is critical to understanding their decisions and actions. Factors such as the desire for approval, the thrill of power, and the fear of failure all play critical roles. A legislator has psychological drivers: power, approval, legacy. The emotional landscape: stress, satisfaction, disillusionment. And personal vs. public: aligning personal beliefs with public actions.

> **Pro Tip:** Develop emotional intelligence. Emotional intelligence can help you navigate the stresses and complexities of building relationships with others. Practice empathy, self-awareness, and effective communication to build strong relationships and make informed decisions.

Section 4: Expectations and Realities – The Dance with Lobbyists

The relationship between legislators and lobbyists is often misunderstood, and sometimes controversial. Legislators expect lobbyists to provide detailed information on a bill's potential impacts and occasional support for their campaigns.

But it is more than providing information giving a perspective on an issue. It is about building rapport with legislators; it's about establishing trust, mutual respect, and a working relationship that benefits everyone involved. In my experience, the key to success isn't simply convincing a legislator to see things my way; it's about building a connection where we can work together as professionals toward shared goals. I've always approached legislators with a simple question in mind: can we depend on each other to get the job done? Whether it's providing them with accurate information, helping them navigate a tough issue, or simply being honest and straightforward, I've found that mutual respect is the foundation of any productive working relationship. And over time, I've learned that being reliable and trustworthy in my role makes it easier for them to rely on me as a resource.

Developing that kind of trust doesn't happen overnight. It requires patience, consistency, and a genuine effort to understand where they're coming from—not just politically, but personally. Some of my strongest working relationships with legislators have been built not in committee rooms but in informal conversations where we connected on a human level. It's in those moments that you figure out whether you can work together and support each other in your respective roles. When trust and respect are present, it's not just about advancing my clients' issues—it's about creating solutions that work for everyone involved. And when those relationships are strong, both sides benefit, because we know we can depend on each other to do the job well. That's what makes the hard work of building rapport so worthwhile. I have a personal code of conduct that I follow that makes it easier for me to maintain my professionalism with legislators, regulators, staff, and contemporaries. My code is as follows:

1. **Always tell the truth.** Trust is the foundation of everything I do.

2. **Present both sides of the story.** Providing a complete picture is essential to the integrity of my work.

3. **Own my mistakes.** If I get something wrong, I will:
   o   Acknowledge the error.
   o   Take responsibility.
   o   Correct it promptly and directly, ensuring the legislator or stakeholder has the right information.

4. **Maintain professionalism.** I treat legislators, colleagues, and staff with courtesy and respect, no matter the circumstances.

5. **Use good manners.** "Please" and "thank you" go a long way—there's a reason my mother taught me that.

6. **Be respectful and helpful.** Relationships matter. I will always offer respect and assistance to those I work with.

7. **Believe in myself and my work.** I trust the value of the issues I represent and the service I provide to my clients.

8. **Protect the process.** I understand my role in upholding the integrity of the legislative process by providing balance, perspective, and accountability.

This code keeps me grounded through both the good times and the challenging ones. It also lets legislators understand that they will be treated with respect and trust during all of our dealings.

Pro Tip: Focus on building mutually beneficial relationships with legislators based on trust, transparency, and shared goals. Clear communication and ethical behavior are essential to maintaining these relationships.

Section 5: From the Other Side – What Lobbyists Expect from Legislators

Conversely, lobbyists have their own set of expectations from legislators. They look for accessibility, predictability, and support for their causes. Understanding these expectations helps one comprehend how legislative support is garnered and the complexities of policy influence.

In my experience, the relationship between a lobbyist and a legislator is built on the same expectations both parties have for one another: accessibility, mutual respect, and trust. These aren't things that come automatically—they have to be earned, day by day and interaction by interaction. I approach every legislator with the same level of professionalism and integrity that I expect in return. My role is not to twist arms or manipulate outcomes; it's to be a resource and an advocate, ensuring that my clients' voices are heard while helping legislators make informed decisions. When both parties meet these expectations, the legislative process becomes not only more productive but also more accountable and transparent, which is what it should always be.

I've encountered my fair share of stereotypes about lobbyists, but I am not—and never have been—"a lowlife lobbyist." I am a professional, and I take pride in representing my clients with honesty, integrity, and respect for the legislative process. My job is to make this complex system manageable, to bridge the gap between my clients and the lawmakers who shape the policies that affect them. That means being accessible when legislators need information, building trust through consistency and follow-through, and respecting the difficult job they have to do. At the end of the day, I'm not just advocating for an issue—I'm helping legislators understand the impact of their decisions and ensuring that the process works as it should: fairly, openly, and with accountability. It's a partnership, and the best results happen when both sides honor that partnership with mutual respect.

Section 6: What Makes an Effective Legislator?

An effective legislator possesses skills, values, and qualities that enable effective governance and meaningful representation. Here are some key attributes that contribute to making a good legislator:

- **Strong Communication Skills:** Effective legislators must communicate clearly and persuasively to convey their ideas, negotiate with other lawmakers, and explain complex issues to their constituents. This includes both speaking and listening skills.

- **Deep Knowledge of Policy Issues:** A good legislator should thoroughly understand the issues that are important to their constituents and the legislative process. This knowledge helps them draft, support, or oppose legislation effectively.

- **Ethical Integrity:** Integrity is crucial in maintaining public trust. Legislators should adhere to high ethical standards, avoid conflicts of interest, and make decisions that are in the best interest of the public rather than personal gain.

- **Problem-Solving Skills:** Politics often involves complex problems that require creative, practical solutions. Effective legislators can identify problems, analyze information, develop viable solutions, and reach out to various informational sources to discover solutions.

- **Empathy and Compassion:** Understanding and genuinely caring about constituents' welfare is vital. This empathy enables legislators to represent the interests of their community effectively and make informed decisions that reflect the needs and desires of the people they serve.

- **Commitment to Public Service:** A strong sense of duty and a commitment to serve the public can motivate legislators to work hard, endure scrutiny, and make difficult decisions.

- **Ability to Compromise:** Politics often requires balancing different interests and making compromises. A good legislator knows how to negotiate and when to give ground to achieve broader goals while still standing firm on crucial principles.

- **Leadership and Vision:** Effective legislators provide leadership on issues and offer a vision for the future that resonates with their constituents. They should be able to inspire and mobilize others toward common goals.

- **Resilience and Perseverance:** Legislative work can be demanding and frustrating. A good legislator needs resilience to overcome setbacks and perseverance to continue advocating for their causes despite challenges.

- **Accessibility and Responsiveness:** It is essential to be available to constituents, listen to their problems, and respond to their needs. Good legislators engage with their constituents regularly and are responsive to their concerns.

Section 7: What Makes an Ineffective Legislator?

While effective legislators possess qualities that promote effective governance and meaningful representation, ineffective legislators often display traits and behaviors that hinder their effectiveness and damage public trust. Here are some characteristics that can make an ineffective legislator:

- **Poor Communication Skills:** Inadequate communication can lead to misunderstandings, ineffective advocacy, and an inability to convey important information to constituents or colleagues.

- **Lack of Knowledge:** A legislator who needs to understand the issues or the legislative process adequately may struggle to contribute effectively to debates, make informed decisions, or respond appropriately to constituents' needs.

- **Unethical Behavior:** Engaging in corrupt practices, lying, or manipulating information for personal gain erodes public trust and undermines the integrity of the office. Such behavior can lead to scandals and distract from legislative duties.

- **Inflexibility and Partisanship:** Being overly rigid or dogmatically partisan can prevent a legislator from effectively collaborating with others, reaching compromises, or considering alternative viewpoints, which are often necessary to achieve legislative success.

- **Lack of Empathy:** Failing to understand or care about the impact of legislation on people's lives can result in policies that harm constituents or fail to address their real needs.

- **Self-Interest Over Public Service:** Legislators who prioritize their own interests, such as re-election, personal power, or financial gain, over the welfare of their constituents, can make decisions detrimental to the public good.

- **Poor Problem-Solving Skills:** Without the ability to analyze problems effectively and develop solutions, legislators may struggle to address the challenges faced by their constituency or the broader community.

- **Inaccessibility and Unresponsiveness:** Ignoring constituent concerns or being unavailable to the public can create a disconnect between the legislator and the people they are supposed to represent, leading to unmet needs and dissatisfaction.

- **Lack of Vision or Leadership:** Without a clear vision or the ability to lead, a legislator may lack direction, be reactive rather than proactive, and fail to inspire or influence others.
- **Low Resilience and Lack of Commitment:** A legislator who quickly gives up in the face of opposition or difficulty or who lacks commitment to their role is unlikely to persist in advocating for essential but challenging policies.

In this chapter we explored the myriad factors that drive individuals to pursue and maintain a political career. From the initial spark of desire to the intricate dance of legislative and lobbying efforts, the life of a legislator is one of constant balance and negotiation. By understanding what motivates politicians, what they expect, and what is expected from them, we can better navigate the complexities of political interactions and influence.

This next chapter discusses the legislative process. Early in my career, I discovered that navigating the legislative process is like mastering a series of challenges, each building on the last. Every preparation phase is critical because you can't skip steps or cut corners. When getting a bill passed, the groundwork you lay before the session even begins is where the battle is won or lost. The more prepared I was, the better my chances of success. It's the difference between watching your bill die and watching it become law.

"The nine most terrifying words in the English language are: 'I'm from the government, and I'm here to help.'"

— Ronald Reagan

Chapter 8: You Want to Change *What?*

"Politics is not a game. It is an earnest business."

—Winston Churchill

You have covered the job of advocate and lobbyist. You have learned how to get registered and stay legal with your regulator. You have also learned to determine which issues are compatible with your internal directive. You now know how to find the perfect client and work with legislators to pursue your issues. And you have learned what makes an effective legislator.

Understanding the legislative cycle is one of the most important skills a lobbyist can master. Once, I underestimated how much timing and preparation impacted the success of a campaign. Each phase of the legislative cycle—drafting, committee hearings, floor debates, and beyond—has its own unique opportunities and challenges. I learned that you can't just show up at the capitol with a good idea and hope for the best; success comes from knowing exactly what must be done in each cycle and planning accordingly. For example, before a session begins, I focus on educating legislators about my client's issues and building relationships with key players who will influence the outcome. This means identifying sponsors, forming coalitions, and developing clear, concise messaging that resonates with lawmakers. The groundwork laid in the early stages often determines whether a bill will gain traction or stall out before it even gets a hearing.

Timing is everything. I've had bills fail not because they lacked merit, but because I tried to push them at the wrong time or didn't build enough support before they reached the floor. A well-crafted strategy includes educating legislators about the issue early, enlisting the right allies to champion the cause, and knowing when to apply pressure and when to let the process unfold naturally. One of the most rewarding parts of this work is seeing the strategy come together— when the coalition you've built shows up in full force, the timing aligns perfectly, and the message you've worked so hard to craft resonates in committee or on the floor. But none of that happens by accident. In this chapter, I'll share my approach to navigating legislative cycles, developing strategies, and building the support needed to turn ideas into law. It's about preparation, timing, and staying one step ahead.

In this chapter you will learn

- About the legislative cycles.
- What must be done in each cycle.
- How to develop strategies.
- How to educate the legislative body about your issues.
- How to identify the players in developing the campaign.
- The timing for the implementation of your legislation.
- How to build support for your issue.

The Ins and Outs of Navigating the Political Maze

Embarking on the path of legislative lobbying is like entering a maze with hidden traps and secret passageways. It's about understanding the basic procedures and grasping the underlying dynamics that propel them. Mastering the ebb and flow of the legislative cycle isn't just beneficial; it's empowering. This cycle mirrors the heartbeat of democracy, requiring active, informed participation for effective influence. Your goal? Elevate your legislative plans from proposals on paper to impactful, actionable strategies.

The journey begins by defining your objectives clearly, aligning your resources with your goals, managing the flow of information meticulously, and ensuring that all activities are navigated within the constitutional and legislative frameworks. You should know your state's constitution. This document is more than historical text; it's your strategic guide to understanding how the legislative structure functions and identifying the best pathways to leverage this knowledge to benefit your clients. This preparation will make you feel confident and ready to navigate the legislative process.

> *Pro Tip:* Read your state's constitution from start to finish. It sets the rules of operation of the state legislature.

Phase One: Legislative Session Segment

The legislative session is where strategy meets action. Limited to a definitive number of days, each session demands precision and preparedness. Here, legislators introduce, debate, and pass laws that shape the public policy landscape. Understanding the unique tempo of your state's legislative session—how many bills are typically introduced and the duration of the session—is not just important, it's crucial for effective campaign planning. Understanding your state's legislative session will give you confidence in your lobbying efforts.

> **Pro Tip:** Outline your legislative campaign down to the smallest detail. The greater the detail you have, the better the planning, will give you more confidence in the successful passage of your legislation.

Navigating the Session

- **Introduction and Assignment:** Every bill's journey begins with being assigned to an appropriate committee. Getting your proposed legislation to the proper committee can significantly influence its success. Picture this stage as the bill's debutante ball; it must make a solid first impression.

- **Committee Hearings:** Committees are where the groundwork you've laid out is tested. This stage is crucial for presenting evidence, garnering support, and making necessary adjustments to the proposed legislation. Think of it as the bill's trial by fire—only the strong and well prepared survive.

- **Floor Debates:** Once a bill clears the committee stage, it faces the broader assembly. This is where broader debates occur, and the strength of your alliances and the persuasiveness of your advocacy are put to the test. Imagine your bill stepping into the coliseum—time to fight the lions (or the opposing party).

- **Crossing the Chambers:** If a bill passes one house, it must then navigate through the other. This phase often requires reiterating the earlier steps but in a new arena with potentially different political dynamics. It's like sending your bill on a cross-country road trip—watch out for unexpected detours and roadblocks.

- **Governor's Desk:** The final hurdle is the governor's approval. Securing the governor's support and navigating this last phase effectively can ensure that your bill becomes law. Think of this as the bill's graduation day—cap, gown, and a signature to make it official.

Pro Tip: Familiarize yourself with the detailed rules of both the house and senate. Understanding these can significantly enhance your ability to navigate the legislative maze effectively. Remember that when your bill gets to the governor's desk, he has three options: veto it, sign it, or let it become law without a signature.

Phase Two: Interim Segment

The interim is your strategic playground. The legislature is out of session, which means no laws are passed, but it is when the groundwork for future legislative battles is laid. Use this time to deepen relationships, reassess the political landscape, and strategize for the next session.

Strategic Planning During the Interim

- **Coalition Building:** Forge alliances with like-minded entities. The strength of your network can amplify your voice and extend your reach. Think of it as building your own Avengers team—each member bringing unique strengths to the table.
- **Research and Strategy:** Delve deep into the issues you champion. Understand every facet, prepare position papers, and plan your advocacy approach. This is your time to play detective—gathering clues, analyzing data, and piecing together the perfect strategy.

- **Legislator Education:** Educate lawmakers on your issues. Organize workshops, provide detailed briefings, and turn legislators into informed champions of your cause. Picture yourself as a teacher in a classroom—educate, enlighten, and empower your students (the legislators).

This period is crucial for keeping your strategy adaptive and responsive to the ever-changing political climate. Maintain robust communication channels with all stakeholders, including ongoing dialogues with the governor's office and legislators who will vote on your issue.

Phase Three: Organizational/Preparation Segment

This final phase before the next legislative session is about precision and preparation. Here, you finalize your plans, secure commitments, and position your legislation for success.

Pre-Session Preparations

- **Sponsorship Lockdown:** Identifying and securing bill sponsors is critical. Choose legislators who are influential, sympathetic to your cause, and capable of swaying others. It's like casting the lead actors for your legislative blockbuster. Pick the ones who will draw the crowds and champion your issue. Early in my career, I thought any legislator would be a good sponsor. That was a big mistake. The sponsor wasn't passionate about the bill, and we got a terrible committee assessment and scheduling. This delayed the bill through the process. It took the whole session to pass the bill and get it to the governor. It was a monumental task to get that bill passed. Lesson learned.

Pro Tip: I cannot stress enough the importance of having the right sponsors for your bill.

- **Bill Drafting and Co-Sponsoring:** Work closely with bill drafters to refine the language and scope of your legislation. Gathering co-sponsors can provide additional support and broaden the bill's appeal. Think of it as fine-tuning your screenplay—every word matters. I learned a hard lesson about the importance of words when drafting legislation when I took it for granted that they knew my issue. I did not review the draft as fully as I should have. As a result, I passed a bill that was incomplete and didn't fully capture the intent of the issue. To correct this situation, I had to run a bill the following year to correct the problem with the original bill.

Pro Tip: Bills are drafted by legislative staff attorneys who do not know your issue. Review your bill closely. In the long run, it will save you time and embarrassment.

- **Leadership and Committee Dialogues:** Establish or strengthen relationships with key leaders and committee chairs. These relationships can be crucial when you need to navigate complex legislative challenges. It's like making friends with the school principal and teachers. Having them on your side makes everything smoother.

Pro Tip: Communication is everything in the legislative process. You can never talk up your issue enough as it moves through the process

As the session approaches, intensify your efforts to align with the governor's office. Early alignment with the executive branch can smooth the path for your legislation and prevent last-minute hurdles.

Building Support for Your Issue

Building support for your issue is akin to running a political campaign. It would be best to win hearts and minds within the legislature and the public.

Steps to Building Support

- **Public Awareness Campaigns:** Use media and public relations strategies to raise awareness about your issue. Social media, op-eds, and public speaking engagements can help you reach a broader audience. Picture this as your campaign trail—get out there and shake some hands (virtually or in person).

- **Grassroots Mobilization:** Engage the community through town hall meetings, petitions, and rallies. Grassroots support can be a powerful tool to show legislators that there is public backing for your issue. Imagine this as rallying the troops—every voice counts.

- **Stakeholder Engagement:** Identify and engage key stakeholders who can influence the outcome of your legislative efforts. This could include business leaders, community organizations, and other advocacy groups. Think of it as building your war council—strategize with the key players.

- **Media Strategy:** Develop a media strategy that includes press releases, media kits, and interviews. Being visible in the media can keep your issue at the forefront of public discussion. Consider this your press junket—spread the word far and wide.

Introducing Your Legislation

Knowing when to introduce your bill, when to push for votes, and when to ramp up public support can make or break your efforts. Timing is critical.

Timing Strategies

- **Session Timelines:** Be aware of the legislative calendar. Know the key dates for bill introductions, committee hearings, and voting sessions. It's like planning a wedding—every detail and date matters.
- **Political Climate:** Assess the political climate. If a hot-button issue dominates the news, waiting until the fervor dies down might be wise. Timing your efforts to avoid political storms can help your bill sail smoothly.
- **Legislative Priorities:** Understand the priorities of the legislative leadership. Aligning your bill with these priorities can increase its chances of success. Think of it as aligning with the stars. Sometimes the right constellation can make all the difference.
- **Strategic Delays:** Sometimes, delaying action to build more support or allow for more favorable conditions might be beneficial. Know when to hold 'em and know when to fold 'em.

The Cycle Continues

Legislative lobbying is cyclical. Each year offers a new opportunity to influence and enact change. Understanding and respecting this cycle can improve your strategies, refine your approaches, and achieve better outcomes. As you gain experience, each phase of the cycle becomes an opportunity to learn from the past and prepare more effectively for the future.

Always remember there is no such thing as too much preparation in lobbying. Your ability to anticipate challenges and plan according-ly can make the difference between success and failure. This expanded insight into each phase of the legislative process provides a compre-hensive understanding of what it takes to be a successful lobbyist. Through meticulous planning, strategic action, and continuous en-gagement, you can navigate the complexities of the political landscape and achieve your legislative goals.

So, arm yourself with knowledge, align your resources, and step confidently into the legislative arena. The game is earnest, the stakes are high, and you can be a powerful force for change with the right strategies. Remember, politics might not be a game, but that doesn't mean you can't play to win.

Next, I'll show you how bold ideas ignite the legislative process and drive public policy forward, walking you through the essential steps to transform your ideas into law.

"Politics is not a bad profession. If you succeed, there are many rewards. If you disgrace yourself, you can always write a book."

— Ronald Reagan

Chapter 9: How Long Does It Take to Shape Public Policy?

"Creating public policy is a multifaceted process that involves balancing competing interests, gathering empirical evidence, and navigating the political landscape. Policy development requires not just technical expertise, but also a deep understanding of public needs, stakeholder engagement, and the ability to anticipate unintended consequences."

—*Diane Ravitch*, Professor at New York University

Shaping public policy is a delicate process, and there are countless opportunities for things to go off the rails along the way. In my experience, no two pieces of legislation are ever the same, and each one demands a tailored strategy to guide it through the maze of the legislative process. A simple one-page bill, for example, can often draw more scrutiny than a complicated, lengthy bill because its brevity makes every word stand out. Lawmakers and stakeholders tend to zero in on the few lines it contains, often sparking intense debate over even the smallest detail. On the other hand, larger, more technical bills may fly under the radar simply because they're harder to fully dissect, though they require just as much care and precision to shepherd through committees and floor debates. Each piece of legislation brings its own challenges, and I've learned that the key is to anticipate potential roadblocks and adapt quickly when the unexpected happens.

Crafting a legislative plan isn't just about strategy—it's about understanding the dynamics of the legislature at that moment in time. Every session has its own unique rhythm, personalities, and priorities, and navigating those requires careful planning and flexibility. For instance, building support for a bill often means knowing when to push hard and when to pull back, when to focus on a specific committee, and when to engage leadership directly. I've also learned that public policy is rarely a straight line; it's a process filled with twists and turns that can require backtracking, revising, and sometimes starting over. But that's also what makes it so rewarding—seeing a bill you've worked tirelessly on make it through the process and become law is a testament to persistence, preparation, and the ability to adapt to whatever challenges come your way.

In this chapter you will learn

- The basics of creating public policy.
- Why legislation passes and fails.
- How to build relationships with legislators.
- About tracking the cost of the campaign.
- Why we are creating public policy.
- Strategies for policy creation.
- About timing and commitment.
- About the process of policy creation.

- The steps in policy creation.

In this chapter we will delve into the essentials of public policy creation, examining why some legislation passes while other proposals fail and exploring the intricate relationships with legislators that can influence these outcomes. Additionally, we'll consider the financial implications of policy campaigns, discuss the underlying motivations for engaging in policy creation, and outline practical strategies, timing considerations, commitment, and the overall process involved.

Section 1: Basics of Creating Public Policy

Creating public policy involves a structured approach to addressing societal issues through strategic planning, advocacy, and mobilization of resources. Here are the fundamental steps involved:

Identifying Issues

The first step in policy creation is identifying the issues that must be addressed. This involves understanding the problem, its root causes, and the affected populations. Who is affected by the issue? Do you have to legislate the problem? Can it be done through a regulatory fix?

Researching the Policy

Conduct thorough research to gather data on the issue. This includes existing policies, past legislative attempts, statistical data, and best practices from other regions or states. Involve stakeholders early in the process and identify quality sponsors for the bill. Remember in chapter 8 I talked about what makes a legislator a good bill sponsor?

Drafting the Proposal

Develop a draft of the policy proposal. This is by far the most important part of the legislative process. You are using it to create public policy that will change the status quo of the legislature and the state's public policy. Your draft must be perfectly written. It should clearly articulate the problem, the proposed solution, and the anticipated outcomes. You do not want to amend the bill through the process because the more it is amended, the more likely the bill will be killed. The bill morphs into something that doesn't do what you want.

Engaging Stakeholders

Engage with stakeholders, including community and industry representatives and other interest groups. Their input is crucial for refining the policy and ensuring broad support. The number of stakeholder groups that should be involved will depend on the issue.

Formulating the Legislative Bill

Once defined, drafted, and vetted by stakeholders, the bill is drafted into a formal piece of legislation ready to be presented to legislators during the session. Remember that the bill is controlled by either the senate or the house leadership in which it will be introduced, and it will be shepherded by the house's prime sponsor(s).

Section 2: Why Legislation Passes and Fails

Various factors can influence whether legislation passes or fails. Understanding these factors is crucial for anyone involved in policymaking, advocacy, or legislative analysis. Politics is messy. Despite our best efforts, sometimes things don't go our way. That is the nature of the beast.

Political Climate and Leadership

- **Alignment with Party Priorities:** Legislation that aligns with the current party's agenda or priorities is more likely to pass. Political leadership often prioritizes bills that fulfill campaign promises or meet urgent public needs.
- **Political Stability:** Stable political environments tend to facilitate smoother legislative processes, while political turmoil or transitions can lead to delays or legislation stalling.

Legislative Relationships and Negotiations

- **Support from Key Legislators:** Bills with the backing of influential lawmakers, including committee chairs or party leaders, often have a higher chance of passing. These legislators can maneuver the bill through tricky legislative processes.
- **Bipartisanship:** In environments where multiple parties must collaborate, bipartisan support can significantly enhance a bill's prospects, especially in divided governments.

Public Opinion and Advocacy

- **Public Support:** Strong public support for an issue can pressure legislators to pass relevant legislation. This is often influenced by media coverage and public opinion polls.
- **Advocacy and Lobbying:** Effective lobbying by interest groups, whether business coalitions, nonprofits, or grassroots movements, can significantly influence legislative outcomes.

These groups often provide expertise, draft provisions, and mobilize public support.

Quality and Scope of Legislation

- **Well-designed Proposals:** Clear, well-researched legislation that effectively addresses the identified problem is more likely to gain support. Ambiguities or poor drafting can hinder a bill's progress.

- **Economic Impact:** Bills with a favorable cost-benefit analysis, or those that do not require substantial public funding, may be more palatable to legislators concerned about budget impacts.

Strategic Timing

- **Legislative Calendar:** The timing of a bill can affect its success. Bills introduced late in a session may not be considered due to time constraints or can be passed late to avoid lengthy debates and minimize opposition to the bill.

- **External Events:** Economic crises, natural disasters, or high-profile incidents can catalyze legislative action in related areas.

Opposition and Controversy

- **Organized Opposition:** Strong opposition from powerful groups can lead to the defeat of legislation. These groups may include business interests, religious organizations, or other influential stakeholders who the legislation might negatively impact.

- **Controversial Issues:** Legislation involving contentious issues, like gun control or abortion rights, often faces significant hurdles due to ideological divisions and societal norms.

> *Pro Tip:* Build a diverse coalition of supporters from various sectors to help bolster your proposal. This broad support base can provide a stronger front against the opposition, particularly in the last few days of the session.

Section 3: Relationships with Legislators

Building and maintaining strong relationships with legislators is essential for influencing policy outcomes. Here are some strategies for effective communication and relationship management:

Regular Communication

Keep in touch with legislators regularly, not just when you need their support. This can be through emails, phone calls, or meetings to update them on relevant issues and progress.

Providing Expertise

Offer your expertise on the issues you are advocating for. Legislators often rely on subject matter experts to understand complex problems and make informed decisions.

Understanding Their Needs

Understand the needs and priorities of the legislators you are working with. Tailor your messaging and proposals to align with their and constituents' interests.

> **Pro Tip:** Be a resource, not a nuisance. Position your-
> self as a valuable resource for legislators. Offer to pro-
> vide data, draft talking points, or organize briefings.
> Avoid overwhelming them with constant requests or
> excessive information.

Section 4: Cost of the Campaign

Public policy campaigns can be expensive, involving research, advocacy, public relations, and lobbying costs. Here's an overview of the
financial aspects to consider:

Budgeting for Research

Allocate funds for data collection, surveys, focus groups, and expert
consultations. High-quality research is the foundation of any successful policy campaign.

Advocacy and Lobbying

Budget for lobbying activities, including travel expenses, conference
registration fees, and possibly hiring professional lobbyists.

Public Relations

Consider the costs of media campaigns, advertising, social media outreach, and the production of promotional materials.

Contingency Fund

Include a contingency fund of 10 to 20 percent of the total budget
to cover unexpected expenses or opportunities during the campaign.

> **Pro Tip:** Leverage in-kind contributions. If you have
> a limited budget, seek in-kind contributions, such as

> donated services, accessible venues, or volunteer labor, to help reduce costs.

I always had my prime sponsor authorize the creation of my client's bill. That way there was no legal expense, and the bill was drafted by the professionals in the legislative drafting office. Ensuring that the bill was drafted correctly 99 percent of the time is one of my tricks of the trade to help clients on a limited budget.

Section 5: Why We Are Creating Public Policy

The motivations behind policy initiatives can vary widely, including addressing specific societal issues, fulfilling political promises, or responding to public demand.

Societal Impact

Policies are often created to address pressing societal issues, such as healthcare, education, or environmental protection. These initiatives aim to improve the quality of life for constituents.

Political Promises

Elected officials may pursue policy initiatives to fulfill campaign promises. These policies reflect their commitments to their voters and their party's platform.

Responding to Public Demand

Public demand can also drive public policy. High-profile issues or crises can prompt swift policy responses to address immediate needs.

> **Pro Tip:** Align with Broader Trends. Align your policy initiatives with broader societal trends and priorities. This alignment can increase public support and make it easier to garner legislative backing.

Section 6: Strategies for Policy Creation

Creating a successful public policy campaign requires a comprehensive strategy integrating various components of advocacy, research, communication, and stakeholder engagement.

Thorough Research and Analysis

- **Foundational Research:** Conduct in-depth research to understand the issue thoroughly, including its causes, stakeholders involved, and previous attempts to address it. This includes data collection, impact studies, and legal reviews.
- **Policy Options:** Develop multiple policy solutions and analyze their potential impacts. This approach allows for negotiation flexibility and tailoring solutions to different stakeholders' needs.

Clear Objectives and Messaging

- **Goal Definition:** Clearly define the policy campaign's goals, ensuring they are specific, measurable, achievable, relevant, and time-bound (SMART).
- **Effective Messaging:** Craft compelling messages that resonate with various audiences. These messages should clearly articulate the problem, the proposed solution, and the policy's benefits.

Broad Coalition Building

- **Diverse Partnerships:** Form alliances with stakeholders who share a common interest in the policy's success, including nonprofits, industry groups, academic institutions, and other influencers.
- **Unified Front:** Ensure all partners align on the campaign's goals and messages. A cohesive coalition enhances the campaign's credibility and reach.

Strategic Advocacy

- **Lobbying:** Engage professional lobbyists or train team members in lobbying to influence policymakers directly through meetings, briefings, and providing expert testimony.
- **Public Advocacy:** Mobilize grassroots support through petitions, public rallies, social media campaigns, and other tools to demonstrate public backing for the policy.

Effective Use of Media

- **Media Relations:** Develop strong relationships with the media to secure coverage that shapes public opinion and influences policymakers.
- **Digital Campaigns:** Use digital platforms, such as social media, blogs, and email newsletters, for wider reach and engagement.

Engagement with Policymakers

- **Continuous Interaction:** Regularly contact policymakers through meetings, updates, and feedback sessions. Being a constant but respectful presence helps keep the policy issue on their agenda.

- **Providing Expertise:** Offer technical and expert support to policymakers, helping them understand the issue deeply and shape their stance based on informed arguments.

Monitoring and Adaptation

- **Track Progress:** Regularly monitor the campaign's progress against predefined milestones and objectives.
- **Flexibility:** Be prepared to adapt strategies based on what is or isn't working, which may involve altering messaging, engaging new stakeholders, or shifting policy proposals.

Evaluation and Learning

- **Assess Impact:** Evaluate the campaign's effectiveness after key milestones and/or at its conclusion, using both qualitative and quantitative metrics.
- **Incorporate Feedback:** Learn from successes and setbacks to refine future strategies and improve the approach for subsequent policy efforts.

> *Pro Tip:* Develop a detailed timeline for your campaign, including key milestones and deadlines. This will help keep the campaign on track and ensure all activities align with the overall strategy.

Section 7: Timing and Commitment

Timing is critical. Understanding legislative calendars and the level of commitment required from stakeholders can make a significant difference.

Legislative Calendars

Familiarize yourself with the legislative calendar, including key dates for bill introductions, committee hearings, and voting sessions. Timing your efforts to align with these dates is crucial for success.

Stakeholder Commitment

Ensure all stakeholders, including coalition partners and supporters, are committed to the campaign. This involves regular communication, updates, and maintaining their engagement throughout the process.

> **Pro Tip:** Policy creation can be a lengthy process. Understand that significant change often takes time and sustained effort, so it's important to be patient and persistent.

Section 8: The Process of Policy Creation

The policy creation process involves several stages, from the initial idea to enactment and implementation. Here's a step-by-step guide:

Idea Generation

Identify the issue and brainstorm potential solutions. Engage stakeholders early in this process to gather diverse perspectives and ideas.

Drafting and Proposal

Draft the policy proposal, incorporating input from stakeholders and experts. Ensure that the proposal is clear, concise, and well researched.

Stakeholder Engagement

Present the draft to stakeholders for feedback. Make necessary revisions based on their input to strengthen the proposal.

Legislative Process

Introduce the proposal to the relevant legislative body. This stage involves lobbying, advocacy, and negotiation to garner support and navigate the legislative process.

Enactment

Once the proposal passes the legislative process, it is enacted into law. This may involve further advocacy to ensure that the executive branch signs it.

Implementation

Work with relevant agencies and stakeholders to implement the policy. Monitor the implementation process to ensure the policy effectively addresses the identified issue.

Evaluation

Evaluate the impact of the policy. Gather data on its effectiveness and identify any areas for improvement.

Pro Tip: Maintain detailed records of all stages of the policy creation process. This documentation could be invaluable for future reference and for assessing the campaign's success.

Next, we dive into the game-changing power of building strong relationships with leadership. I quickly learned that the closer your ties to the leaders of both houses, the more effective you become as a lobbyist. With solid connections, your bills get more favorable attention, you land top-tier sponsors, and your committee assignments are strategic. Simply put, representing your clients becomes much smoother when you've got leadership in your corner.

> "Governments don't want a population capable of critical thinking. They want obedient workers. People just smart enough to run the machines and just dumb enough to passively accept their situation."
>
> — George Carlin

Chapter 10: Who's Really in Charge?

"Effective public policy at the state level requires
close collaboration with legislative leaders. They
have the experience, the relationships, and the understanding of the political landscape that can make
or break a policy initiative. Building strong partnerships with these leaders is essential to navigating the
complexities of the legislative process and turning
good ideas into law."

—*Tom Daschle*

A t the start of every legislative session, I made it a priority to send out an information sheet about my company and the clients I represented. This sheet included an overview of my company, a list of all my clients for the session, the key issues they cared about, and my contact information. Two weeks before the session began, I would personally deliver this packet to every legislator, ensuring they had everything they needed to understand who I was and what my clients stood for. It was a simple yet effective way to put my name, my company, and my clients in front of legislators before the whirlwind of the session began. It also gave me the chance to set the tone for open communication and accessibility right from the start.

A few days after delivering the information sheets, I would follow up with the leadership of each house to see if they had any questions about my clients or their legislative priorities. These conversations were invaluable—not just for addressing specific concerns, but for re-establishing relationships with leadership and nurturing those connections for the months ahead. It was a great way to remind them that I was a resource they could rely on and that my clients' issues mattered. This small effort paid off in big ways, keeping my company and clients top of mind not only with leadership but with every legislator. It was an investment in relationships that helped pave the way for effective advocacy throughout the session.

In this chapter you will learn

- The roles of state senate and house leadership.
- The intricacies of working with leadership to get your bill positioned.
- The value of legislative relationships and how they can affect outcomes.

The Power Players of the Senate

The state senate is a complex and powerful body within the legislative framework. Understanding the roles and strategies for engaging with legislative leadership can significantly impact the success of your policy initiatives.

President of the Senate

The president of the senate is more than just a ceremonial figure; they are central to the legislative process. Holding the gavel, the president controls the pace and order of legislative business daily. From an insider's perspective, their power to assign bills to committees can make or break legislative priorities. They strategically shape what the senate discusses and when, often aligning these decisions with broader political strategies.

> **Pro Tip:** To engage effectively with the senate president, understand their legislative priorities and frame your communications to demonstrate how your interests can support their agenda. Building rapport based on mutual interests can pave the way for more meaningful interactions.

President Pro Tempore

The Senate President Pro Tempore in a state legislature holds a vital leadership position, serving as a key figure in guiding the legislative process and ensuring the Senate operates effectively.

> **Pro Tip:** Again, this is a key individual that you must know on a first name basis. This individual fill in when the President of the Senate is unavailable, helps with the administration of the Senate, and is involved in committee assignment of the members and bill assignment to the various committees.

Senate Majority Leader

The senate majority leader is often seen as the chief strategist for the majority party. They are responsible for the legislative agenda, coordinating the debate schedule, and ensuring that key bills have the votes needed to pass. This leader is key in negotiating with the minority party and orchestrating the majority's response to legislative proposals.

> **Pro Tip:** Timing is crucial when dealing with the majority leader. Approach them when they are setting the legislative calendar to get your issues on the agenda early. Also, understand the party's pressure points and propose solutions that align with the leader's goals to get their attention.

Senate Minority Leader

The minority leader's role is pivotal in providing checks and balances within the senate. They lead the opposition against the majority party's proposals and strive to amplify the minority party's voice in legislative decisions. Their influence often lies in their ability to sway public opinion and mobilize votes for or against key legislation.

> **Pro Tip:** Effectively lobbying the minority leader requires offering them tools that enhance their negotiating power. Provide data, expert testimonies, and public support that can help them make a compelling case on the floor.

Senate Committee Chairmen

Committee chairmen wield considerable influence over the fate of legislation within their specific domains. They decide which bills to bring forward for hearings and which to set aside, controlling the detailed legislative agenda in their expertise. Their role is crucial in shaping the legislation that ultimately reaches the floor for a vote.

> **Pro Tip:** To influence committee chairmen, offer comprehensive briefs that include potential impacts, expert opinions, and public sentiment. Being seen as a resource can make your interactions more productive and your positions more likely to be considered.

House Leadership

The house of representatives is another critical legislative body where strategic interactions with leadership can determine the success of policy proposals.

Speaker of the House

The speaker of the house is one of the most influential figures in state politics. This role involves presiding over house proceedings and playing a significant strategic role in legislative planning and coordination. The speaker's ability to appoint committee members and chairs also gives them substantial leverage over legislative outcomes.

> **Pro Tip:** Regular communication and demonstrating broad support for your issues are key strategies when engaging with the speaker. They need to see not just the merits of an issue but also its support across constituencies to prioritize it.

Speaker Pro Tempore

The **Speaker Pro Tempore** serves as a key leader in the House of Representatives, stepping in for the Speaker of the House when necessary and assisting with legislative operations.

> **Pro Tip:** This individual is the number two person in House leadership. Get to know them and become

their new best friend. They can expand your opportunities to interact with the Speaker of the House.

House Majority Leader

The house majority leader acts as the tactical arm of the majority party, ensuring that legislation endorsed by the party moves smoothly through the house. They are instrumental in rallying party members during key votes and in negotiating compromises with the opposition when necessary.

> *Pro Tip:* Be clear and concise in your dealings with the majority leader. Provide actionable solutions and be ready to show how these align with the party's broader objectives to garner support.

House Minority Leader

In the house, the minority leader is tasked with consolidating the minority party's stance and crafting alternative strategies to the majority's proposals. Their influence can be critical in close votes, where they can tip the balance by swaying a few key members.

> *Pro Tip:* Supporting the minority leader with strategic information and expert backing can help amplify their voice. Focus on how your cause can appeal to undecided members and provide the minority leader with the ammunition to argue effectively.

House Committee Chairmen

Like their senate counterparts, house committee chairs control the trajectory of legislation in their realms. They facilitate discussions, manage committee votes, and play a significant role in refining legislative details.

> **Pro Tip:** Success with house committee chairmen often comes from early engagement. Get involved at the committee stage to shape the debate before it reaches the floor. Offering detailed, well-researched positions can help secure a chairman's backing.

Committee Staff

Committee staffers play a crucial role in the legislative process, often serving as the backbone of policy development and decision-making within the state legislature. These dedicated professionals conduct in-depth research, draft legislation, and analyze complex issues, providing the detailed information lawmakers rely on to make informed decisions. They coordinate hearings, gather expert testimony, and synthesize diverse viewpoints, ensuring committee members comprehensively understand the topics. Additionally, staffers liaise between committee members, stakeholders, and the public, facilitating communication. They assist the committee chair in scheduling and conducting the committee hearing and parliamentary procedures associated with the conduct of their hearing. They are a source of information for lobbyists regarding their legislation in a scheduled committee hearing.

Lobbying Tactics: Working the System

Lobbying involves more than just understanding the legislative process; it's about navigating the personalities and politics within. Here's how seasoned lobbyists work the system to influence policy:

Building Relationships

Strong, ongoing relationships with key legislators are the foundation of effective lobbying. Engage with them consistently, not just when you need a favor.

> **Pro Tip:** Schedule regular check-ins with legislators to maintain and strengthen relationships. This builds trust and ensures they are familiar with your issues.

Offering Solutions

Legislators are problem solvers by nature. When you approach them, come with solutions, not just problems. Be ready to explain how your proposals can benefit their constituents.

> **Pro Tip:** Always present data and real-world examples to support your solutions. This makes your proposals more compelling and easier for legislators to back.

Utilizing Timing

Timing can be everything. Understanding the legislative calendar and knowing when to push for your issues can greatly enhance your chances of success.

> **Pro Tip:** Monitor the legislative schedule closely and identify key dates for bill submissions, hearings, and votes. Plan your lobbying efforts around these critical times.

Creating Coalitions

Building broad-based coalitions can amplify your influence. When legislators see diverse support for an initiative, they are more likely to consider it seriously.

> **Pro Tip:** Include a variety of stakeholders in your coalition, such as community groups, industry leaders, and other advocacy organizations. This broadens your support base and strengthens your position.

Real-World Examples

Illustrate your points with success stories and case studies. Showing real-world impacts can make a compelling argument for your cause.

> **Pro Tip:** Develop a portfolio of case studies that highlight successful outcomes related to your issue. This can be a powerful tool in persuading legislators.

By mastering these tactics, lobbyists can effectively steer the legislative process toward outcomes that benefit their clients while contributing to sound public policy.

The Value of Legislative Relationships

Building strong relationships with legislators is crucial for successful lobbying. These relationships are built on trust, mutual respect, and ongoing engagement.

Trust and Reliability

Legislators need to know they can trust your information and support. Being a reliable source of data and assistance builds a strong foundation for future interactions.

> **Pro Tip:** Always provide accurate and timely informa-tion. If you commit, follow through to build credibility.

Mutual Respect

Respecting legislators' roles and responsibilities fosters a positive working relationship. Acknowledge their challenges and work collab-oratively to find solutions.

> **Pro Tip:** Approach legislators with respect and under-standing. Avoid being overly aggressive or demand-ing, which can damage the relationship.

Ongoing Engagement

Maintaining regular contact with legislators keeps your issues top of mind and demonstrates your commitment to working with them.

> **Pro Tip:** Send periodic updates on your issues, includ-ing any new developments or data. This keeps legis-lators informed and engaged.

Mastering Legislative Influence

Understanding and navigating the legislature requires a deep appre-ciation of the structural and interpersonal dynamics. Each leadership position, from the president of the senate to the house committee chairmen, offers unique opportunities and challenges for those look-ing to influence policy.

The insider tips help you effectively engage with these power players. Whether you're a lobbyist, an advocate, or simply a citizen interested in state politics, knowing who holds power, what motivates them, and how to approach them can make all the difference in your legislative endeavors.

Ultimately, successfully navigating the legislative landscape is about more than just making connections; it's about making the right connections at the right time with the right approach. By applying these insider strategies, you will enhance your influence and contribute to shaping policies that reflect the needs and aspirations of the people you represent.

"One-fifth of the people are against everything all the time."

— Robert F. Kennedy

Chapter 11: Understanding the Language of Legislation

"To make good decisions, you must first understand the rules of the game—reading the bill is how you learn the rules. Reading a bill isn't just about understanding the words—it's also about uncovering the intentions, implications, and potential consequences behind them."

— Unknown

In the early years of my career, I made the mistake of scanning bills rather than reading them in their entirety. I would skim through, looking for anything that immediately jumped out as relevant to my clients. If nothing caught my eye, I'd move on to the next piece of legislation, thinking I had done enough. That approach worked—until it didn't. One particular bill made it through committee without raising any red flags, but after it passed, my client pointed out a single sentence buried deep in the text that could seriously harm his company. To my embarrassment, I had missed it entirely. The damage wasn't irreversible. I scrambled to amend the bill on second reading in the house to fix the issue, but in that moment, I looked like an amateur. It was a hard lesson to learn, but one that has stayed with me ever since.

From that point forward, I made it a rule to read every bill word for word, from beginning to end. No skipping, no assumptions, no shortcuts. I've learned that the devil truly is in the details, and even the smallest clause or phrase can have massive implications. It's easy to overlook a seemingly minor provision, but those details are often the ones that can jump out and derail everything. Understanding a bill fully is the foundation of effective advocacy. It guides your strategy, strengthens your credibility, and ensures you can represent your clients with confidence. That one humiliating experience early in my career taught me the value of diligence and attention to detail. If there's one piece of advice I'd pass along, it's this: Read the bill. Every single word. Every single time.

In this chapter you will learn

- How to read a bill.
- The unwritten intent of the bill.
- The significance of the sponsors and the committee assignment of the bill.
- The unintended consequences of the bill.

Understanding the language of legislation is not just a matter of curiosity; it's a key to empowerment and understanding the back story of the bill, a crucial part of the legislative process. If you can't read the bill, you can't fully comprehend what it attempts to put into statute. Legislative language is unique in laying out the idea the sponsor tries to put into law. It's a format unlike any other and understanding it can be a fascinating journey. There is a unique format that all legislative drafters follow in writing the legislation. Remember, each state has its rules for writing legislation, but every state has these essential components in its legislation. By understanding these components, you become a more informed and active participant in the legislative process.

Components of State Legislation

- **(A) Session Identification:** This identifies the session in which the legislation is drafted, introduced, and acted on.

- **(B) Drafter Information:** At the state level, legislation is usually drafted by the state's legislative counsel or legal staff, often in consultation with legislators or outside advocacy groups. Sometimes, legislators may play an active role in drafting the bill, especially in smaller states.

- **(C) Bill Number:** Each bill introduced in a state legislature is assigned a number for tracking purposes. This number is typically assigned by the clerk's office when the bill is filed, and it will differ depending on whether it's introduced in the state house or the state senate. The bill number represents the house where it originates. For example, in Colorado, house bills start at 1000 (HB24-1001), and senate bills begin at 1 (SB24-01)

- **(D) Sponsorship:** The house and senate sponsors of the legislation are listed. Each piece of legislation has a primary sponsor, typically the legislator responsible for introducing the bill. Multiple co-sponsors can also support the bill. At the state level, it's common for bills to have both house and senate sponsors.

- **(E) Committee Assignment(s):** This is the committee to which the bill is assigned. Once a bill is introduced, it is referred to the appropriate committees based on its subject matter. These committees hold hearings, make amendments, and determine whether to move the bill forward for a total vote in the state legislature. Each chamber (house and senate) will typically have its own committees.

- **(F) Title:** The bill's title concisely describes its purpose or the issue it seeks to address. A title must be specific in identifying the single issue of the bill. State laws often have shorter, more functional titles than federal legislation.

- **(G) Summary of the Bill:** A summary provides a brief overview of what the proposed legislation will do. The summary highlights the bill's key goals, impacts, and mechanisms and is designed for legislators and the public to understand its main provisions at a glance.

  From here we get into the nuts and bolts of legislation. Each bill is unique. Its idea, implementation, funding, and which part of the bureaucracy is responsible for the management of the legislation.

- **Preamble/Legislative Declaration (Optional):** Some bills include a preamble or legislative declaration, which provides the legislative intent and reasoning behind the proposed law. This section is optional and can help clarify the bill's purpose for future interpretation by courts or agencies.

- **Definitions:** The definitions section clarifies the meaning of key terms or phrases used throughout the bill. This is crucial for avoiding ambiguity and ensuring the law is applied consistently.

- **Findings or Purpose:** The findings section presents the evidence, facts, or rationale for the legislation, helping to establish the legal basis for why the law is necessary. The purpose section outlines what the bill seeks to accomplish.

- **Main Provisions or Operative Clauses:** The main provisions (sometimes called operative clauses) lay out the specific changes the legislation will make. This is the bill's core and details what it will do, who it will affect, and how it will be enforced.

- **Scope and Applicability:** This section specifies who and what is affected by the bill should it become law, including the geographic areas, industries, or individuals impacted. It clarifies the scope of the law's enforcement.

- **Procedures and Implementation:** This section details how the bill will be implemented, and which state agencies or departments will oversee it. It may also include specific procedures or timelines for rolling out the provisions.

- **Enforcement Provisions:** The enforcement section describes how the law will be monitored and enforced. It outlines the penalties, fines, or other actions that will be taken against those who violate the law.

- **Funding Mechanism (Appropriations):** This section explains how the state government will allocate the necessary resources if the bill requires funding. This could involve creating a fund, reallocating existing resources, or imposing taxes or fees.

- **Sunset Clause or Expiration Date (Optional):** Some state bills include a sunset clause, depending on what the bill is trying to do. This clause sets a specific expiration date for the law. This ensures that the law is periodically reviewed and must be reauthorized if necessary.

- **Severability Clause:** A severability clause ensures that if one part of the law is found to be unconstitutional or invalid, the remaining provisions can still stand.
- **Effective Date:** The effective date specifies when the law will come into force. State laws typically take effect upon the governor's signature or at a future date specified in the bill.
- **Amendments or Repeals:** If the bill modifies or repeals existing state laws, this section identifies which laws are being amended or repealed and how.

Now that you know how a bill is drafted, you'll better understand how it affects your client. The devil is in the details, and misinterpreting the bill can create unanticipated consequences for the people you represent. Read it and understand it to avoid making changes throughout the process.

Our next chapter explores the journey of promoting and passing legislation. We'll explore how each step affects a bill, from introduction to getting to the governor's office, focusing on the roles and strategic moves essential for successfully navigating this path.

"Instead of giving a politician the keys to the city, it might be better to change the locks."

— Doug Larson

Second Regular Session Seventy-
fourth General Assembly STATE
OF COLORADO

(A)

INTRODUCED

LLS NO. 24-0913.01 Shelby Ross x4510 (B)

HOUSE BILL 24-1146 (C)

HOUSE SPONSORSHIP
Bird and Taggart, Sirota

SENATE SPONSORSHIP
Bridges and Zenzinger, Kirkmeyer

(D)

House Committees   Senate Committees
Appropriations

(E)

A BILL FOR AN ACT

CONCERNING AUTHORIZING THE DEPARTMENT OF HEALTH CARE
POLICY AND FINANCING TO SUSPEND A PROVIDER'S
ENROLLMENT IF THE PROVIDER IS PARTICIPATING IN AN
ORGANIZED FRAUD SCHEME.

(F)

Bill Summary (G)

*(Note: This summary applies to this bill as introduced and does
not reflect any amendments that may be subsequently adopted. If this bill
passes third reading in the house of introduction, a bill summary that
applies to the reengrossed version of this bill will be available at
http://leg.colorado.gov.)*

Joint Budget Committee. The bill authorizes the department of
health care policy and financing (state department) to suspend the
enrollment of a medicaid and children's basic health plan (programs)

Chapter 12: **Blueprint for Legislation**

"Legislation is the art of the possible. It requires careful drafting, building consensus, and understanding the nuances of both the issues and the people involved. Success in passing laws depends on knowing how to listen, negotiate, and sometimes compromise, but always keeping your eye on the ultimate goal."

— Bill Bradley

D rafting legislation is one of the most challenging aspects of working in the legislative process. It might seem straightforward to outline the content of your bill and lay out the problem you're trying to solve, but the real challenge lies in choosing the right words—words that can't be misinterpreted or twisted in ways you didn't intend. What might seem clear and concise to you as the drafter can end up confusing others or failing to address the issue you're trying to solve. I've learned the hard way that even a single word can change the entire meaning or scope of a bill, sometimes with unintended consequences. It's frustrating to think you've nailed down the language only to realize later that it needs to be reworked because it's either too vague, too broad, or too narrow.

I once had to go through four separate drafts of a bill just to get it right. Each time I thought we were done, but after reviewing it with stakeholders and legal counsel, we found gaps or ambiguities that could create problems down the line. The process felt endless, but it taught me a valuable lesson: drafting legislation is as much an art as it is a science. It takes patience, attention to detail, and the humility to admit when something isn't working. You can't rush it, and you can't skip steps, because the words you choose will live on far beyond the bill's passage. When it comes to drafting legislation, precision is everything. Take the time to get it right—it's worth every edit.

In this chapter you will learn

- The roles of state senate and house leadership in managing legislation.
- The delicate job of writing legislation that captures your intent.
- The intricacies of working with leadership to get your bill positioned.
- The value of legislative relationships and how they can affect outcomes.

Section 1: Introduction: Understanding Legislation and Public Policy

Legislation is the cornerstone of public governance, transforming ideas into the laws that shape our society. But what exactly is public policy? In essence, it encompasses the decisions and laws that govern our daily lives, reflecting the needs, values, and priorities of a community. Understanding the complex process by which an idea evolves into enforceable legislation is crucial for anyone involved in or affected by the crafting of public policy.

This chapter will provide an insider's guide to the lifecycle of legislation, from its inception as a mere concept to its final form as a written piece ready for legislative consideration. We'll explore the critical role of strong legislators who sponsor and champion these bills, the strategic involvement of leadership in both houses, and the optimal timing for introducing legislation.

We will delve into strategies for identifying supporters and opponents, which are essential for navigating the often-turbulent waters of the legislative session. By understanding these foundational elements, stakeholders—from citizens to seasoned lobbyists—can influence the legislative process more effectively.

In addition, we will break down each stage of this process, providing key insights and practical advice from seasoned insiders. This chapter aims to equip you with the knowledge and strategies needed to effectively engage with and impact the legislative process.

Section 2: Key Players: The Importance of Strong Legislators and Sponsors

Characteristics of Effective Legislative Sponsors

The success of legislation heavily depends on the charisma and clout of its sponsor. Effective sponsors are not only knowledgeable and passionate about the bill's subject but also possess the political savvy necessary to navigate the legislative process. They must be adept at building coalitions and persuading colleagues across the aisle.

Pro Tip: If you're advocating for legislation, align yourself with legislators who are respected by their peers and have a track record of legislative success. Their endorsement can significantly boost your cause.

How Sponsors Influence the Legislative Journey

Sponsors play a pivotal role throughout the legislative process. They introduce the bill, argue its merits in committee meetings and floor debates, and work tirelessly behind the scenes to drum up support or negotiate amendments.

Pro Tip: Maintaining a strong, supportive relationship with your bill's sponsor is crucial. Regular updates, expressions of appreciation, and public support can help keep the sponsor engaged and motivated.

Section 3: Engaging Leadership: Leveraging Influence in Both Chambers

The Strategic Importance of Involving Legislative Leaders

Getting the buy-in of key leaders in both the senate and house can dramatically increase a bill's chances of success. These leaders can expedite a bill's progress by prioritizing it within the legislative agenda or guiding it through potential roadblocks.

Pro Tip: Early engagement with leadership can help you understand the legislative priorities and potential resistance you might face. Tailoring your strategy to align with leadership's goals can make your advocacy more effective.

How Leaders Can Expedite or Hinder Legislation

Leadership has the authority to assign bills to favorable or less favorable committees, influence scheduling for hearings, and even advocate directly to the executive branch. Their support or opposition can be a game-changer.

> **Pro Tip:** Cultivating relationships with leadership involves demonstrating how your legislation can serve broader political objectives or party goals. Being able to articulate these benefits clearly and convincingly is key.

Section 4: Timing and Strategy: When to Introduce Legislation

Best Practices for Timing the Introduction of Bills

The timing of a bill's introduction can significantly impact its viability. Introducing a bill early in the session can allow more time for discussion, amending, and passage, while introducing it during a time of relevant public interest or after a related event can increase its visibility and perceived urgency.

> **Pro Tip:** Monitor the legislative calendar and current events closely. Timing your bill's introduction when it aligns with public attention or legislative priorities can enhance its chances of success.

Section 5: Navigating Support and Opposition

Identifying and Consolidating Support

Identifying potential allies early in the process is crucial. Support from influential advocacy groups, constituents, and other legislators can build momentum for a bill. Engaging these supporters through coordinated advocacy efforts can strengthen your position.

> **Pro Tip:** Use town hall meetings, social media campaigns, and direct lobbying to rally support. Demonstrating broad backing for your initiative can be persuasive in legislative debates.

Understanding and Preparing for Opposition

Anticipating opposition is equally important. Understanding the arguments and concerns of opponents can help you prepare counterarguments or negotiate compromises.

> **Pro Tip:** Engage directly with potential opponents to understand their concerns. Early dialogue can sometimes mitigate opposition or even transform opponents into supporters through thoughtful amendments.

Section 6: Strategies for Success: Pushing Legislation Through

Legislative success requires a multifaceted strategy that includes diligent preparation, strategic timing, robust advocacy, and sometimes complex negotiation. Employing a combination of direct lobbying, public advocacy, and strategic compromises can navigate a bill through the tumultuous waters of legislative debate to eventual passage.

> **Pro Tip:** Be adaptable and prepared for long-haul ef-
> forts. Legislation often requires multiple sessions to
> pass, and persistence is key. Stay engaged with your
> legislative contacts, keep your supporters mobilized,
> and always be ready to revise your strategies based on
> legislative feedback and shifting political landscapes

Section 7: Detailed Steps to Passing Legislation

Idea Generation and Stakeholder Engagement

The legislative process begins with identifying a need or problem. This can come from various sources, including citizens, advocacy groups, businesses, or government agencies. Once the idea is formulated, engaging stakeholders is crucial. This means reaching out to those who will be affected by the legislation, gathering their input, and building a coalition of support.

> **Pro Tip:** Host workshops and public forums to gather
> diverse perspectives. This not only strengthens the
> bill but also builds a network of supporters who can
> advocate for it.

Research and Drafting

Thorough research is essential to ensure the proposed legislation is effective and enforceable. This involves studying existing laws, understanding the legal implications, and consulting experts. The drafting process should incorporate this research to create a robust and clear proposal.

> **Pro Tip:** Utilize the resources of legislative research
> offices and legal advisors. Their expertise can help
> avoid pitfalls and enhance the quality of the bill.

Finding a Sponsor

A strong legislative sponsor is vital. The sponsor is the primary advocate for the bill, responsible for introducing it to the legislature and guiding it through the process. They must be committed and have the political clout to garner support.

> *Pro Tip:* Approach legislators who have a history of supporting similar issues or who have expressed interest in your cause. Their prior engagement can be a valuable asset.

Committee Assignment and Hearings

Once a bill is introduced, it is assigned to a committee that specializes in the bill's subject area. The committee reviews the bill, holds hearings to gather information and opinions, and makes amendments if necessary.

> *Pro Tip:* Attend committee hearings and provide testimony. Bringing in experts or affected individuals to testify can provide compelling support for the bill.

Debating and Voting

After passing through the committee, the bill is debated on the floor of the legislature. Legislators discuss its merits and drawbacks, propose further amendments, and finally, vote on it.

> *Pro Tip:* Prepare for the debate by briefing legislators on key points and counterarguments. Ensuring they have all the information they need can help secure their vote.

The Role of Lobbyists and Advocacy Groups

Lobbyists and advocacy groups play a crucial role in the legislative process. They provide information, advocate for or against bills, and mobilize public support. Effective lobbying involves building relationships with legislators, understanding their interests, and presenting a clear and persuasive case for your position.

> **Pro Tip:** Build long-term relationships with legislators and their staff. Consistent engagement and providing reliable information can establish you as a trusted advisor.

Passage and Implementation

Once the bill passes both houses of the legislature, it is sent to the executive (e.g., the governor) for approval. Upon signing, the bill becomes law. The final step is ensuring effective implementation, which may involve working with government agencies to develop regulations and monitor compliance.

> **Pro Tip:** Stay involved after the bill is passed. Helping with the implementation phase can ensure the law achieves its intended impact and allows you to address any issues that arise.

Section 8: Challenges and Pitfalls

Navigating the legislative process is fraught with challenges. Political opposition, bureaucratic hurdles, and shifting public opinion can all pose significant obstacles. Being prepared for these challenges and having strategies to address them is crucial for success.

Anticipating Opposition

Understanding who might oppose your bill and why is essential. This allows you to prepare counterarguments and consider compromises that can address opponents' concerns without undermining the bill's objectives.

> **Pro Tip:** Engage with potential opponents early. Sometimes, opposition arises from misunderstandings that can be resolved through dialogue.

Adapting to Changing Circumstances

The political and social landscape can change rapidly. Being adaptable and ready to adjust your strategy in response to new developments is key to maintaining momentum and support for your bill.

> **Pro Tip:** Regularly reassess the political climate and be flexible in your approach. Staying nimble can help you navigate unforeseen challenges.

The Journey of Legislation

Creating and passing legislation is a complex, dynamic process that requires strategic thinking, persistent effort, and a deep understanding of the legislative landscape. By mastering the steps outlined in this chapter—from idea generation to implementation—you can effectively influence public policy and contribute to meaningful change.

"Politicians and diapers have one thing in common:
they should both be changed regularly, and for the
same reason."

— Unknown

Chapter 13: Follow the Yellow Brick Road

"Passing legislation is a multi-step process. It starts with an idea, followed by drafting a bill, gaining sponsors, and then shepherding it through committee hearings and debates. Afterward, you must build support in both houses, work out differences, and finally, get it to the president's desk. It's never easy, but persistence and coalition-building are key."

—*Tip O'Neill, Man of the House*

N avigating the legislative process is much like traveling down the Yellow Brick Road in *The Wizard of Oz*—it's full of unexpected challenges, shifting dynamics, and key moments where every step matters. Early in my career, I believed the process was straightforward: introduce a bill, present a strong argument, and let the votes take care of themselves. But I quickly learned that the journey is far more complex and often unpredictable. A bill can face resistance at any stage—whether in committee, during floor debates, or even through behind-the-scenes negotiations—and understanding how to address these obstacles is critical. I've worked on bills that seemed unstoppable at introduction only to hit a roadblock in committee when stakeholders raised unforeseen concerns. On the flip side, I've salvaged bills others had written off by finding the right allies or making strategic concessions to keep them alive. The key is knowing how to adapt at each step while staying focused on the ultimate goal.

Each stage of the legislative process plays a vital role in determining the fate of a bill, and mastering these stages is essential to success. From the moment a bill is introduced, you need to understand who the key players are—sponsors, committee chairs, stakeholders—and how to work with them effectively. Committee hearings can be especially critical, as they serve as the proving ground where you must make your case and address any opposition. I've spent hours refining talking points and rallying coalitions to ensure a bill's message resonated at this stage. Then there's the final push on the floor, where timing, votes, and even the relationships you've built earlier in the session can make or break your efforts. In this chapter, we'll break down the legislative process step by step, exploring the strategies, relationships, and decisions that are essential for guiding your bill to success. With a clear roadmap and the right approach, even the most challenging legislative path can be conquered.

In this chapter you will learn

- The fundamental steps in the legislative process.
- The importance of initial documentation and sponsorship.
- Strategies for favorable committee assignments.
- The significance of the fiscal note.
- How to schedule a committee hearing.
- The role of bill sponsors in committee.

- Strategies for when votes are lacking.
- Insights into the importance of strategy and preparation.

Section 1: Introduction: The Journey Begins

Every step in this process, from the initial drafting and introduction to the strategic navigation through committees, plays a critical role in the bill's fate. Understanding these steps not only demystifies the legislative process but also equips sponsors and advocates with the knowledge to influence outcomes effectively.

Section 2: Bill Introduction and Initial Steps

Process of Introducing a Bill

The process begins when a bill is formally introduced in the legislature. This step requires a sponsor, typically a legislator who believes in the bill's purpose and is willing to champion it. The bill is assigned a unique number, which will be used to track its progress through various stages.

Importance of Initial Documentation and Sponsorship

Initial documentation must be meticulously prepared. This includes the bill text, justifications for the legislation, and any supporting documents that bolster the bill's intent. Choosing the right sponsor is crucial; their influence and commitment can significantly affect the bill's journey through the legislative maze.

> **Pro Tip:** Select a sponsor with strong connections within key committees and proven advocacy skills. Their ability to navigate political dynamics and garner support will be invaluable.

Section 3: Committee Assignments: Navigating the Maze

How Committee Assignments Are Determined

The assignment of a bill to a particular committee is one of the most pivotal moments in its legislative journey. This decision is typically made by the speaker of the house or the president of the senate, depending on the chamber in which the bill is introduced. The nature of the bill—its subject matter, scope, and the interests it affects—guides this assignment. Leaders also consider the political implications, such as the potential for controversy or significant impact, which can influence which committee is chosen.

> *Pro Tip:* Building a good relationship with the speaker of the house or the president of the senate is crucial. Understand their priorities and how your bill aligns with them. This knowledge can be leveraged to secure a favorable committee assignment, easing the bill's path.

Strategies for Ensuring Favorable Committee Assignment

Strategically, it's essential to lobby for a committee whose chair and members may be sympathetic to the bill's goals. Legislators often seek assignments to committees that align with their expertise or interests, which can be used to predict their voting behavior on specific issues.

> *Pro Tip:* Before the bill is introduced, discuss it with potential committee members to gauge their interest and possibly secure early support. Providing detailed briefings can also help win their favor early in the process.

Section 4: The Fiscal Note: Balancing the Books

Explanation of the Fiscal Note and Its Importance

A fiscal note is an official analysis that estimates the financial impact of the proposed legislation on the state's budget. It assesses the costs, savings, revenue gains, or losses associated with the bill's implementation. This step is crucial as it provides lawmakers with an understanding of the economic implications of passing the bill. The fiscal analysis is done by legislative staff.

Steps in Creating a Fiscal Note

1. **Data Collection:** Gathering relevant financial data and cost estimates.

2. **Analysis:** Evaluating the direct and indirect economic impacts.

3. **Report Preparation:** Documenting the findings in a clear and concise format.

4. **Review and Approval:** Submitting the report for review by budget committees and relevant legislative bodies.

> *Pro Tip:* Engage with financial analysts and budget experts early to ensure accurate and favorable fiscal analysis. Presenting a well-prepared fiscal note can significantly boost your bill's credibility and support.

Section 5: Scheduling for Committee Hearing

How and When a Bill is Calendared for Its Committee Hearing

After a bill is assigned to a committee, it must be scheduled for a hearing. This is where the bill is discussed and debated and where public testimonies are heard. The timing of this scheduling can be influenced by several factors, including the legislative calendar, committee workload, and the priorities set by committee chairs.

Factors Influencing the Scheduling

- **Legislative Calendar:** Understanding the session timeline and key deadlines.

- **Committee Priorities:** Aligning your bill's importance with the committee's agenda.

- **Strategic Timing:** Scheduling during heightened public interest or following relevant events.

> **Pro Tip:** Communicate regularly with the committee chair's office to stay updated on the scheduling status. Offering to provide detailed information and support can help prioritize your bill for early hearings.

Section 6: Role of Bill Sponsors in the Committee

How Sponsors Advocate for the Bill in Committee

The sponsor plays a vital role in advocating for the bill during committee hearings. They present the bill, explain its purpose, and argue its merits. Influential sponsors also address committee members' questions and concerns, providing clear and convincing responses.

Strategies for Obtaining an Accurate Committee Vote

- **Pre-Hearing Briefings:** Meet with committee members beforehand to discuss the bill and address potential concerns.

- **Expert Testimonies:** Bringing in experts and stakeholders to testify in support of the bill.

- **Negotiations:** Be open to amendments and compromises to secure additional votes.

> **Pro Tip:** Prepare a compelling presentation with visual aids, real-world examples, and strong supporting evidence. This can help make your case more persuasive and memorable.

Section 7: When the Votes Aren't There

What to Do if You Don't Have Enough Votes to Pass the Bill Out of Committee

If it becomes apparent that there aren't enough votes to pass the bill out of committee, don't panic! Several strategies and recourses are available to revive or modify the bill to garner the necessary support.

- **Amendments:** Propose changes to the bill that address the concerns of undecided or opposing members.
- **Compromise:** Find a middle ground with key stakeholders to build broader support.
- **Public Pressure:** Mobilize grassroots support to pressure committee members through calls, emails, and social media campaigns.

Recourses Available for Reviving or Modifying the Bill

- **Reintroduction:** If you don't get the bill passed the first time, introduce a revised bill version in the next legislative session.
- **Alternate Committees:** Seek reassignment to a different committee that might be more favorable.
- **Building Coalitions:** Partner with influential organizations and individuals to strengthen advocacy efforts.

> **Pro Tip:** Sometimes, no matter what you do, the bill will not pass out of committee; the votes are just not there. Let this be a teaching moment. Learn from it. Keep detailed records of the concerns and objections raised during the committee hearing. Use this information to refine your strategy and address these issues directly in your future attempts.

Section 8: Detailing The 8 Steps of Bill Creation – Bill Roadmap

We have covered the basics of policy creation, the factors that influence legislative success, and the importance of strong relationships with legislators, permitting stakeholders to navigate the complexities of the political landscape effectively. Let's take a deep dive into the eight steps of bill creation.

Step 1: Public Policy Idea

Public policy can originate from various sources:

- Constituents
- Legislators
- Business owners
- Existing public policy
- Anywhere there is an issue that needs a legislative solution

Questions that need to be answered:

- Is there a need for this legislation?
- What issue does it address?
- What problem does it solve?
- Who are supporters?
- Who is the opposition?

All the questions need to be answered before you can proceed.

Step 2: Identifying Stakeholders and Sponsors

Stakeholders need to be identified, contacted, and willing to support your issue and can include:

- Association groups
- Business groups
- Chamber of commerce
- Social advocates
- Legislators

Some strong legislative sponsors are legislators who:

- agree with your issue.
- have a bill title available (legislators have a limited number of bills they can introduce).
- know your issue and are passionate about the issue.
- agree to carry your bill.

Step 3: Draft Legislation

When drafting legislations, you need to work with your client and other stakeholders:

- Outline your bill.
- List the significant points of the bill.
- Prepare your legislative draft for your sponsor. (This doesn't have to be in legislative format.)

The sponsor of your bill will be either a representative or a senator. The sponsor determines in which chamber the bill will originate. If you have a sponsor from both houses, one will be the prime sponsor, and the other will be the co-sponsor. The prime sponsor determines which house the bill originates from.

- Get authorization from your sponsor to have legislative drafters write your bill.
- Meet with the drafter and explain your bill so there is an understanding of what they are writing up.
- Review draft with client, stakeholders, and sponsor(s).
- Approve the draft of the bill and have your sponsor(s) give the okay to print the bill.
- Discuss with your sponsor(s) the best committee to hear the bill. (Sponsor(s) can request that the bill be assigned to a particular committee with leadership.)

Step 4: Legislation is introduced for action by the legislature

Depending on which chamber the bill will be introduced, the following occurs:

- The bill is introduced to the body.
- It is given a bill number.
- It is assigned to a committee.
- The bill is placed on the committee schedule for action.

Step 5: The Committee Hearing

The following must occur to prepare for the upcoming committee hearing:

Prior to the Hearing

- Prepare a fact sheet on legislation. The fact sheet explains the legislation, what the issue is, and how the legislation is a solution to the issue. Identify the opposition and give their arguments against the bill

- Identify committee members, research their backgrounds, schedule meetings to discuss legislation, and ask for support.
- Identify individuals who will provide testimony at the hearing.
- Practice your committee testimony so you are comfortable with the message you will deliver. You will have a short time to testify, so make sure your message is concise and drives your point home with the committee.
- Work with your sponsor(s). They will have already talked to committee members and will have an opportunity to hear their feelings about his bill.
- Count committee votes, who supports and doesn't support the bill. Concentrate on those who do not support the bill. Attempt to change their mind. You need to know if your bill will pass the committee before going into the committee hearing.

Day of the Hearing

- Get there early. Give yourself some time to discuss any last-minute issues before the hearing.
- Once in the committee room, register to testify.
- The committee chairman will announce your bill and call people to provide testimony after your sponsor has explained the bill.
- When testifying, remember that the committee members want to hear your story. They will be polite and try to make you feel comfortable. They want you to convince them why they should vote for your bill.
- When the testimony is complete, the sponsor will come back to answer any questions and ask for their favorable vote.

- The vote will be taken, and the committee will determine the fate of the bill.

Step 6: Second Reading of the Bill

After the bill passes out of committee, it goes to the body that introduced it. The bill is placed on the calendar for the second reading, and the full body acts on it at its scheduled date and time.

Before the Second Reading

- Mobilize the grassroots network of the client and stakeholder groups. Have the network send emails and make calls to all the legislators.
- Distribute the fact sheet to all the legislators.
- Make capitol visits to legislators to discuss the bill, answer any questions, and ask for their support.
- Count the votes. You must have a majority of the body to pass the bill.
- Work with your sponsor. Have the sponsor talk to members who have not decided on the legislation. Have your sponsor check to see if any amendments will be offered. If there are amendments, get a copy of the amendment and talk to the legislator who will be offering it. Can you live with the amendment? Have a fallback position that you can accept.

Second Reading Debate. They will:

- Have the sponsor come to the podium and explain the bill
- Other body members come to the podium and explain their support or opposition or offer amendments.

- The voice vote is taken after the debate. The chairman of the body declares whether the bill passes or fails.

Section 7: Third Reading and Final Passage of the Bill

After the second reading, the bill is calendared for the third and final reading. The support or lack of support is pretty much known. But things happen between the second and third reading. You must be prepared and follow through to make sure the bill passes.

Supporters and Stakeholders, before Third Reading, need to:

- Mobilize the grassroots network of the client and stakeholder groups. Have the network send emails and call all the legislators, reminding them to support the legislation.
- Count votes. You must have a majority of the body to pass the bill
- Work with your sponsor. Have the sponsor take the pulse of the body to ensure passage.

The leadership calls up the bill for a third reading. He will:

- Have the sponsor come to the podium and make a statement about the bill
- Other members come to the podium and explain their support or opposition.
- The vote is called, and a recorded vote is taken. The body's chairman declares whether the bill passes or fails after the vote is tallied.

After passing one house, the bill is sent to the other house for action, and the process repeats. After passing both houses, the bill is sent to the Governor for final action.

Step 8: The Governor

Once the bill passes both houses, the governor will finalize the process. The Governor has three options. He can:

- Sign the bill into law
- Let the bill become law without his signature
- Veto the bill

Supporters, Stakeholders and sponsors need to:

- Mobilize the grassroots network of the client and stakeholder groups. Have the network send emails and call the Governor asking for his support
- The bill's sponsors need to interact with the governor to ensure he signs the bill

Section 8: Lessons from the Road

The journey of running legislation is as intricate as the Yellow Brick Road, filled with predictable patterns and unexpected detours. Successfully navigating this path requires strategic planning, building strong relationships, and maintaining flexibility to adapt to changing circumstances.

Throughout this chapter, we've explored the key stages in the legislative process, from the initial introduction and sponsorship of a bill to the critical roles of committees and fiscal analysis. We've discussed the importance of strategic timing, effective advocacy, building coalitions, and maintaining persistence, even when the path becomes challenging.

By understanding these steps and applying the insider tips provided, you can significantly enhance your ability to guide legislation through the complex maze of the legislative process. Remember, the journey may be long and filled with obstacles, but with careful planning, strategic alliances, and unwavering determination, you can turn your legislative goals into reality.

Now, let's talk about what happens when you lose the bill. Losing a bill is a gut-wrenching experience. It's the culmination of hard work, strategy, and hope, all coming to a halt with a single vote or decision. The frustration of seeing your efforts fall short, coupled with the disappointment of not delivering for your clients or cause, can be overwhelming. There's a sense of loss that lingers, knowing you fought hard but didn't get across the finish line. Yet, amid the setback, it often sparks a renewed sense of purpose—a drive to analyze, adapt, and return even more prepared for the next fight.

"Passing legislation is a lot like making sausage: you might enjoy the result, but you definitely don't want to see how it's made."

— Attributed to Otto von Bismarck

Chapter 14 : How to Kill the Bill

"Killing bad legislation is as important as passing good legislation. Sometimes, the best way to protect the public interest is to stop harmful policies before they become law."

—Ralph G. Neas

A dvocacy isn't just about passing legislation. It's equally about protecting your clients interests by defeating bills that could harm them. One of the most memorable battles of my career was over a bill that the casinos were pushing hard, but it would have had devastating consequences for charitable gaming, specifically bingo. I knew this was a fight I couldn't lose, so I threw everything I had into stopping the bill. Three separate times during the session, I thought we had killed it only to see it resurrected through parliamentary procedure. Each time, it required regrouping, re-strategizing, and rallying support to block it again. It was exhausting, but the stakes were too high to let up for even a moment.

When the bill finally made it to the governor's desk, I knew that this was my last chance to stop it. I reached out directly to the governor's office, presenting clear, well-reasoned arguments for why this bill was harmful and why a veto was necessary. The stakes couldn't have been higher. I had done everything I could, and now it was out of my hands. Thankfully, our arguments were sound, and the governor vetoed the bill, effectively saving bingo and protecting charitable gaming. That experience taught me that advocating for a client often means fighting just as hard to stop bad legislation as you do to pass good legislation. Persistence, strategy, and solid arguments make all the difference, especially when the odds feel stacked against you. Sometimes, the win is in what you prevent from happening.

In this chapter you will learn

- How to identify bad legislation.
- The back story of the legislation.
- How to develop the campaign.
- How to develop strategies.

There will come a time when you must kill legislation for your client. It's part of the legislative process. As we all know, not all legislation is created equal; sometimes a bill can do you more harm than good, mainly if it goes against your clients' interests and goals. You kill legislation through a campaign of research, planning, strategy, and mobilization of your legislative assets. There are no guarantees that you will be successful, but if you have a well-thought-out campaign, it can be accomplished. Let's examine the process.

Identifying the Legislation

You have identified legislation introduced during the session. You know your client has an issue with what has been introduced. Here are the steps to get the background and help you build your campaign to defeat the bill.

- **Read and study the bill.** Cross-reference the citations highlighted in the bill. Gain a complete understanding of what the bill is all about and how it affects your client.

- **Check the bill's sponsors.** This will tell you a lot about the support for the legislation. Is the bill sponsored by leadership, a committee chairman, or a body member? Are there sponsors from both chambers? This will tell you a lot about the degree of support for the legislation.

- **Determine the committee assignment.** What committee has it been assigned to? Does the bill's intent match the appropriate committee area of oversight? If this doesn't match up, it tells you the degree to which leadership supports the legislation.

- **Talk to the sponsors.** You must talk to the sponsors to determine who is behind the legislation. Why did they bring it to the sponsor? What is the reason for bringing the legislation forward? What issue is creating the legislation?

> **Pro Tip:** In my experience, sponsors may not be forthcoming with all the information. But this is your first step in researching the issue. Glean as much information from them as you can.

- **Contact the lobbyist representing the group.** Ask them about the issue. Ask them for any material on the issue, fact sheets, white papers, or anything they share with legislators to support their issue.

- **Is there a fiscal note?** Most proposed legislation has costs associated with its intent.

Pro Tip: If the bill has a cost, this will be important information you can use in your campaign to oppose it.

- **Check legislative history.** See if this issue has been raised in previous legislative sessions. If it has been raised in different sessions, what were the reasons for it not passing? Check the voting records to find out who supported and opposed the bill.

Pro Tip: Voting records will tell you a lot. You can find the voting records in the journals for the house and senate for the appropriate session. There may still be legislators who acted on the bill in previous sessions. You can contact them and gather useful information for your campaign.

This may seem like a lot of work. But the more information you have, the better your campaign will be designed to defeat the legislation.

The Campaign

You have done your research. You know the reasons for the bill and who is behind it, and you understand their strategy for passing it. Now, it's time to put together your campaign to defeat it. Here are the steps you must take to get it done:

- **Identify your reasons for opposing the bill.** After reviewing the bill, list your reasons for opposing it. Be specific but concise in identifying each reason. This will help you formulate your message to the legislators.

- **Create your strategy.** You must develop your message and plan how you will lobby committee members, the legislative body, and the governor's office. You must also decide when to activate your grassroots and what they will communicate to the legislators.

- **Develop your message.** Since you know the proponent's issue, have reviewed their materials, and talked to the sponsors, you have the intel to craft your message to counteract their strategy for passing their bill. Make sure your message rebuts their arguments and demonstrates why their legislation isn't needed. Share your message with your coalition members and your grassroots contacts. Remember to check if the bill has a fiscal note attached to it. Use this in your messaging.

- **Identify like-minded groups.** Build a coalition and work collectively to interact with committee members (the committee to which the bill was assigned), other legislators, and the governor's office. Present your fact sheet and other materials that show that the legislation is not necessary

- **Work the committee members.** Talk to each member and find out where they are on the bill. Share your information. Find out who supports and who opposes the bill. The goal is to kill the bill in committee. If this doesn't happen, you must work the floor to stop the bill.

Pro Tip: When killing a bill, the ideal situation is to kill it in committee. You have fewer members to influence, and if it gets out of committee, you must lobby the whole body to oppose the bill.

- **Count committee votes.** Counting votes helps identify committee members who need extra attention to change their votes in your favor. When the day comes that the committee hears the bill, you need this information to identify people who will testify and what they will say in their testimony.

> *Pro Tip:* I have lost opportunities to kill a bill in committee by not counting votes, which is a critical step in killing the bill. This means counting committee, second reading, and third reading votes in each house as the bill makes its way through the process. Count your votes!

If the bill passes the committee, your next task is to kill it when the whole body acts on it. Follow your campaign strategy, pull out all the stops, and work the body to kill the bill. Adjust your strategy as circumstances dictate so you can modify your plan to fit the situation. Remember, there are six opportunities to defeat the proponent's legislation (committee, second reading, third reading): three times in the House and three times in the Senate (unless the bill has more than one committee assignment, there are two committee opportunities). The last and final opportunity is with the governor. He has the final say on whether a bill becomes law. In all instances, the goal is to kill the bill early in the process.

Now, let's talk about what happens when you lose the bill. Losing a bill is a gut-wrenching experience. It's the culmination of hard work, strategy, and hope, all coming to a halt with a single vote or decision. The frustration of seeing your efforts fall short, coupled with the disappointment of not delivering for your clients or cause, can be overwhelming. There's a sense of loss that lingers, knowing you fought hard but didn't get across the finish line. Yet, amid the setback, it often sparks a renewed sense of purpose—a drive to analyze, adapt, and return even more prepared for the next fight.

"Losing a bill feels a lot like dropping your ice cream cone: all that effort, and now it's a mess nobody wants to deal with."

— Unknown

Chapter 15: What Does it Mean We Lost the Bill?

"Success is not final; failure is not fatal: It is the courage to continue that counts."

—Winston Churchill

Losing a bill is one of the hardest experiences in advocacy. I've seen bills fail for a variety of reasons. Sometimes the importance of the legislation wasn't clear enough to lawmakers, or we underestimated the opposition's ability to frame the debate. Other times, a client's lack of understanding of the complexities of the legislative process made it challenging to address concerns or pivot quickly when unexpected obstacles arose. Losing a bill carries an emotional impact, not just for me but for my clients, who often end up frustrated and disappointed. It's tough to see a bill you've worked so hard on stall in committee, die on the floor, or fail to make it to the governor's desk. Early in my career, I would take these setbacks personally, feeling like I'd let my clients down. But I've learned that failure is often part of the process, and the best thing to do is take a step back and ask What can I learn from this?

When a bill fails, it's an opportunity to reflect and refine. I analyze the factors that contributed to the defeat: Was the message unclear? Did we fail to build enough support? Were there unforeseen dynamics that we didn't prepare for? I've found that turning legislative defeat into eventual victory requires a willingness to regroup, learn from the setback, and develop a stronger plan for the future. For example, one bill I had to run four times before it passed and was signed by the governor. The bill failed because it was perceived as a threat to the general contractor's association. We simplified the language, built better coalitions, and reframed the issue, ultimately securing its passage. Legislative losses can be painful, but they are also opportunities to grow, strategize smarter, and come back stronger. Advocacy is a long game, and every setback is just another step toward achieving the ultimate goal.

In this chapter you will learn

- To accept your defeat.
- How to analyze what went wrong.
- How to review what you could have done better.
- To turn defeat into victory.

Losing Legislation

It was a bright, sunny, crisp January afternoon in Colorado. The eleven-member House State Affairs Committee had a full agenda, and the room was packed with individuals waiting to testify on their bills. Our bill was number two on the agenda. This bill pitted the large general contractors against the subcontractors on a contractual issue.

Before the hearing, I had gotten our group of supporters together. I briefed them on how to testify, rehearsing their stories to demonstrate to the committee the importance of the legislation before them.

Finally, our bill was up. The opposition went first to give their testimony. Five people testified. Questions were asked. Our group went next. Each of our eleven individuals told their stories supporting the bill. Committee members asked them questions. Testimony ended. The committee discussed the bill. The chairman called for the vote. The staffer called on each committee member for their vote. The vote was 11 to 0. The bill was dead! We all got up and left the room defeated. The chairman called up the next bill on the agenda.

Section 1: What Happened?

1. What did the legislators not understand?

Legislators often need help fully comprehending proposed legislation's technical intricacies and nuanced implications. A bill's language can be convoluted, and key points may be missed without a comprehensive explanation. Moreover, the broader context or the specific problems the bill aims to address may need to be more effectively communicated. Given the sheer volume of bills and issues they face, it's a challenge for legislators to delve deeply into each one.

> **Pro Tip:** Explain complex issues using visual aids and straightforward language. A concise, well-crafted executive summary can help make your points clear and memorable.

2. Why did they not understand the importance of the legislation?

The legislation's importance might have needed to be adequately highlighted amidst competing priorities. Legislators might have yet to see a direct connection to their constituents' needs or their policy agendas. Furthermore, the lack of compelling data or testimonials demonstrating the bill's impact could have contributed to this misunderstanding. Without seeing the tangible benefits or consequences, legislators might downplay its significance.

> **Pro Tip:** Align the bill's goals with the legislators' agendas and highlight how the bill will specifically benefit their constituents. Personalize the impact with local examples and success stories.

3. Why do you feel bad about losing the bill?

Losing a bill can be disheartening for several reasons. As a lobbyist, you invest significant time, effort, and resources into advocating for legislation. You build relationships, craft strategies, and passionately present your case. When a bill fails, it can feel like all those efforts are in vain. Additionally, you may feel you've let down your client, who trusted you to navigate the legislative process and secure a favorable outcome.

> **Pro Tip:** Acknowledge the emotional toll but use the loss as a learning opportunity. Reflect on what went wrong and how to improve future efforts.

4. How do you explain losing to the client?

Clients often have a personal or professional stake in the legislation and may not fully appreciate the complexities of the legislative process. They might assume that the bill's importance is self-evident, not realizing that legislators need clear, concise, and compelling arguments to prioritize it. This disconnect can lead to frustration and confusion on the client's part when their expectations aren't met.

> **Pro Tip:** Keep clients informed throughout the process. Regular updates and clear explanations can help manage their expectations and give them a realistic view of the challenges. Do not hold back on telling the client the good, the bad, and the ugly of the process.

Section 2: What Went Wrong?

1. Insufficient Communication

Perhaps the key points were not communicated effectively to the legislators. Legislative language can be dense and difficult to navigate, making it easy for crucial elements to be lost in translation.

> **Pro Tip:** Simplify your message. Use bullet points and highlight the most critical aspects of the bill. Ensure that your key points are easily digestible and repeat them often.

2. Lack of Advocacy

There might not have been enough advocacy or lobbying efforts to keep the bill in legislators' minds. Continuous engagement is crucial to remind legislators of the bill's importance.

> **Pro Tip:** Maintain a presence. Frequent interactions with legislators and their staff can keep your bill at the top of their mind. Even small touchpoints, like emails or brief check-ins, can make a big difference.

3. Timing Issues

The bill could have been introduced when other issues were dominating the legislative agenda. Timing is crucial in legislative advocacy.

> **Pro Tip:** Research the legislative calendar and plan the introduction of your bill when it's likely to get the most attention. Avoid times when legislators are preoccupied with more pressing issues.

4. Opposition

Strong opposition from other interest groups or legislators could have swayed the decision. Understanding and mitigating opposition is essential.

> **Pro Tip:** Engage with potential opponents early. Sometimes opposition arises from misunderstandings that can be resolved through dialogue. If not, be prepared to counter their arguments effectively.

5. Legislative Strategy

The strategy employed might not have been the most effective in garnering the necessary support. Legislative success often requires a multifaceted approach.

> **Pro Tip:** Develop a comprehensive strategy that includes coalition building, media engagement, and direct lobbying. Be flexible and ready to adjust your approach as needed.

Section 3: What Could We Have Done Better?

1. Better Education

More comprehensive briefings and educational sessions for legislators to ensure they understand the bill's importance.

> **Pro Tip:** Host informational sessions or workshops. These can provide legislators with a deeper understanding of the bill and its implications, making them more likely to support it.

2. Stronger Coalition Building

Building a broader coalition of supporters to advocate for the bill, demonstrating wider community or industry backing.

> **Pro Tip:** Identify and engage key stakeholders early. Diverse support can lend credibility and weight to your advocacy efforts. Regularly update and involve your coalition in advocacy activities.

3. Improved Communication

Crafting clearer, more compelling messages and using data and personal stories to highlight the bill's impact.

> **Pro Tip:** Use a mix of quantitative data and qualitative stories. Numbers can show the scope of the problem, while personal stories can make it relatable and urgent.

4. Enhanced Engagement

Engaging with legislators more frequently and effectively, ensuring they are updated with relevant information and developments.

> **Pro Tip:** Create a communication plan. Schedule regular updates and check-ins with legislators and their staff to keep them informed and engaged.

5. Strategic Timing

The introduction and promotion of the bill should align with legislators' agendas and the current political climate.

> **Pro Tip:** Timing is everything. Introduce your bill when it's likely to receive the most attention and support. Monitor political trends and legislative priorities to find the optimal moment.

6. Counteracting Opposition

Identifying and mitigating opposition early by addressing concerns and countering arguments.

> **Pro Tip:** Prepare a comprehensive opposition analysis. Understand the arguments against your bill and develop counterarguments and solutions to address them.

Section 4: Turning Defeat into Victory

Despite the initial failure, we did not give up. We ran the bill for the subsequent three sessions. We successfully got the bill to the governor's desk in the next two sessions. Both times he vetoed it. Finally, during the next session, with a new governor who supported the subcontractors, the bill was signed into law. We changed public policy concerning the contractual relationship between general contractors and subcontractors.

The journey to legislative success is often long and fraught with setbacks. However, persistence, strategic adjustments, and learning from past mistakes can turn initial failures into ultimate victories.

> *Pro Tip:* Don't be discouraged by setbacks. Use them as opportunities to refine your strategy and strengthen your resolve. Persistence pays off in the legislative process.

Learning from Loss

In legislative advocacy, the path to success is often paved with lessons learned from failure. Understanding why a bill was lost is crucial, as it highlights the gaps in communication, strategy, and engagement that must be bridged to transform defeat into future victories.

Reflecting on the experience of losing a bill offers valuable insights:

- **Communication:** Ensure that your message is clear, compelling, and consistently reinforced.
- **Education:** Invest time in educating legislators and stakeholders about the bill's importance and impact.
- **Engagement:** Maintain regular, meaningful engagement with legislators, stakeholders, and supporters.
- **Adaptability:** Be flexible and ready to adjust your strategy in response to new information and changing circumstances.
- **Persistence:** Never give up. Legislative success often requires multiple attempts and continuous advocacy.

This quote at the beginning of the chapter underscores the importance of reflection and learning from the setbacks experienced in the legislative process. Reflecting on these points can provide valuable insights and strategies for future legislative efforts, helping to turn a loss into a learning opportunity.

By understanding these steps and applying the insider tips provided, you can significantly enhance your ability to guide legislation through the complex maze of the legislative process. Remember, the journey may be long and filled with obstacles, but with careful planning, strategic alliances, and unwavering determination, you can turn your legislative goals into reality. Getting legislation passed is all about perseverance, tenacity and never giving up.

The next part of the legislative puzzle is about playing nice with others. Working with other lobbyists in the legislature often balances collaboration and competition. While you may represent different interests, forming alliances with fellow lobbyists can be essential to advancing shared goals or defeating opposing legislation. Building these relationships requires trust, open communication, and a deep understanding of each other's objectives. At times, you may find yourself working closely with those you typically compete against, pooling resources and strategies to sway key decision-makers. Ultimately, success in the legislative arena often depends on the strength of these professional networks and the ability to find common ground.

"Losing a bill is like a pizza delivery arriving without the pizza—everyone's confused, disappointed, and still hungry for results."

— Unknown

Chapter 16: All We Need is Love – Collaborating with Lobbyists

"Working with other lobbyists is crucial for building coalitions and expanding influence. By collaborating, you can share information, coordinate strategies, and present a united front, which significantly increases the likelihood of success in influencing legislation."

— *Allan J. Cigler*

I n the complex and often fast-paced world of legislative lobbying, collaboration is a key element for success. Lobbying is not a solitary endeavor; it involves a dynamic interplay of various stakeholders, each with their own interests, strategies, and influences. Whether advocating for policy changes, securing funding, or protecting your client's interests, working effectively with other lobbyists can make the difference between achieving your goals or falling short.

We'll explore the different types of lobbyists you'll encounter, from public lobbyists representing state government departments to professional lobbyists hired by private interests and volunteer lobbyists championing grassroots causes. Understanding the roles and motivations of these different actors is crucial and empowering in forming effective alliances and advancing your objectives.

We will then discuss practical strategies for building and maintaining relationships, from networking basics to sophisticated coalition-building techniques. However, we understand that conflicts are inevitable. We'll also cover effective communication, conflict resolution, and professional conduct. These tools will equip you to manage both collaborative efforts and unavoidable conflicts. With these strategies, you'll be prepared and capable of handling any situation, ensuring your confidence and control in the legislative arena.

Finally, we will address the challenging scenario when collaboration isn't possible due to irreconcilable differences or past conflicts. Learning to navigate these situations professionally and strategically ensures you remain influential and respected.

Through real-life case studies and insider insights, you will gain the knowledge and skills necessary to thrive in the legislative arena. By the end, you'll have a comprehensive understanding of working with other lobbyists to achieve shared success while maintaining your integrity and advancing your goals.

In this chapter you will learn about

- The landscape.
- The different types of lobbyists.
- Building relationships.
- Strategic collaboration.
- Communication skills.
- Conflict resolution.
- Handling irreconcilable differences.

Section 1: Understanding the Landscape

Navigating the legislative arena requires a keen understanding of the landscape, including the key players, how influence is distributed, and the dynamics of competition and cooperation. This section provides a roadmap for identifying your allies and competitors and understanding the power structures that shape legislative outcomes.

Know Your Allies and Competitors

In any legislative environment, knowing who is who is essential. This means identifying those who share your interests and goals and those who might oppose them. Start by creating a comprehensive list of lobbyists and organizations within your area of interest. Categorize them based on their positions and potential impact on your initiatives.

> **Pro Tip:** Attend industry events, follow legislative updates, and engage in conversations to stay informed about key players. Establish a routine of monitoring these developments to keep your knowledge current.

Understanding the motivations and strategies of other lobbyists can help you anticipate their actions and identify opportunities for collaboration. For example, if you know that a particular lobbyist is focused on healthcare reform, and your interest aligns with theirs, you can approach them for a potential alliance.

Mapping the Influence

Once you have identified the key players, the next step is to map out their influence. Influence in the legislative arena can stem from various sources, including relationships with lawmakers, expertise in specific policy areas, and the ability to mobilize public opinion.

Create a visual map or a detailed list that outlines who holds sway over which issues. This should include:

- **Legislative Committees:** Identify which lobbyists have strong ties to influential committees and their members.
- **Key Legislators:** Note which lobbyists have established relationships with legislators who are pivotal to your interests.
- **Public Opinion Leaders:** Recognize lobbyists who can effectively sway public opinion and media coverage.

> *Pro Tip:* Seasoned lobbyists often have long-standing relationships with key legislators and staff. These relationships are built over years of consistent interaction and mutual benefit. Observing and learning from these veterans can provide valuable insights into building your influence.

Assessing the Political Climate

Understanding the broader political climate is also crucial. This includes being aware of the current legislative priorities, political alliances, and the overall mood of the legislative body. Factors such as upcoming elections, shifts in party control, and major policy debates can influence lobbying efforts.

> *Pro Tip:* Stay attuned to the political climate by regularly reading political news, attending public hearings, and participating in policy discussions. A solid grasp of the context in which you operate will help you tailor your strategies more effectively.

Building Your Influence

In addition to understanding the landscape, it's important to actively work on building your influence. This can be achieved through various means:

- **Establishing Expertise:** Position yourself as an expert by providing valuable insights, data, and testimony on relevant issues.

- **Developing Relationships:** Build and maintain relationships with legislators, their staff, and other lobbyists. Consistent, reliable interaction fosters trust and opens doors for collaboration.

- **Engaging in Coalitions:** Participate in or form coalitions around common goals. Working with a group can amplify your voice and increase your influence on critical issues.

- **Political Parties:** Integrate with political party leadership. Go to fundraisers. Hold fundraisers for legislatures. Do whatever is necessary to be seen and recognized for your assistance with party activities.

By thoroughly understanding the landscape and strategically building your influence, you can effectively navigate the legislative arena, identify opportunities for collaboration, and advance your objectives.

Section 2: Types of Lobbyists

Various types of lobbyists populate the legislative arena, each representing different interests and employing distinct strategies. Understanding the roles and motivations of these different actors is crucial for effective collaboration and competition. In this section, we'll explore the three primary types of lobbyists: public, professional, and volunteer.

Public Lobbyists

Public lobbyists represent various departments and agencies within state government. Their primary role is to advocate for the interests and needs of their respective departments, working to secure funding, influence policy decisions, and ensure that their departments' goals are represented in legislative discussions.

Characteristics of Public Lobbyists:

- **Government Employees:** Often, public lobbyists are state or local government employees tasked with promoting the interests of their departments.
- **Policy Experts:** They possess deep knowledge of specific policy areas and government operations, making them valuable sources of information and expertise.
- **Focus on Public Interest:** Their advocacy is typically aligned with the broader public interest and the operational needs of government entities.
- **Insider Insight:** Building relationships with public lobbyists can be highly beneficial, as they often have direct access to key legislators and can provide valuable insights into the intricacies of government operations and policies.

Professional Lobbyists

Private interests such as corporations, trade associations, and other organizations hire professional lobbyists. Their primary goal is to shape legislation, regulation, and public policy to benefit their clients' interests. These lobbyists are typically highly skilled in negotiation, persuasion, and strategic communication.

Characteristics of Professional Lobbyists:

- **Hired Advocates:** They work for clients who pay for their services, ranging from large corporations to industry groups.
- **Broad Networks:** Professional lobbyists often have extensive networks within the legislative and regulatory communities.
- **Resource-Rich:** They usually have significant resources, including research, data, and communication tools, to support their advocacy efforts.

> *Pro Tip:* Professional lobbyists can be powerful allies or formidable opponents. Building relationships with them can provide access to valuable information, resources, and strategic support for shared goals. You will have your adversaries, that is the nature of the process.

Volunteer Lobbyists

Volunteer lobbyists represent grassroots organizations or advocate for specific issues out of personal passion or commitment. Unlike their public and professional counterparts, volunteer lobbyists often operate with limited resources but bring high dedication and authenticity to their advocacy efforts.

Characteristics of Volunteer Lobbyists:

- **Passion-Driven:** Their advocacy is motivated by a deep personal commitment to a cause or issue.

- **Resource-Constrained:** They often lack the financial resources and institutional support that public and professional lobbyists have.
- **Grassroots Focus:** Volunteer lobbyists frequently organize, mobilize public support, and draw media attention to their causes.

> *Pro Tip:* Collaborating with volunteer lobbyists can enhance your credibility and bring a sense of authenticity to your advocacy efforts. Their passion and grassroots connections can be powerful assets in building public support and influencing policymakers.

Navigating Interactions with Different Types of Lobbyists

Understanding the different types of lobbyists and their unique characteristics can help you navigate interactions more effectively. Here are some tips for working with each type:

- **Public Lobbyists:** Leverage their expertise and access to government information. Collaborate on issues where public and private interests align.
- **Professional Lobbyists:** Utilize their resources and networks. Look for opportunities to form strategic alliances that benefit both parties.
- **Volunteer Lobbyists:** Support their grassroots efforts and harness their passion for your initiatives. They help in areas where they may lack resources.

By recognizing and appreciating the different roles and strengths of public, professional, and volunteer lobbyists, you can build more effective collaborations and navigate the legislative arena with greater confidence and success.

Section 3: Building Relationships

Building strong relationships with fellow lobbyists is essential for success in the legislative arena. Effective networking, professionalism, and strategic coalition-building are all key components of fostering these relationships.

Networking Basics

- **Effective Networking:** Networking is the foundation of building relationships in the legislative arena. Here are some tips for effective networking:

- **Attend Events:** Regularly attend industry conferences, legislative sessions, and social events where lobbyists gather. These venues provide valuable opportunities to meet and interact with your peers.

- **Be Approachable:** Approach networking with an open and friendly attitude. Be genuinely interested in others and their work.

- **Follow-up:** After meeting someone new, follow up with a brief email or message to solidify the connection. A simple "It was great meeting you" can go a long way.

- **Maintain a Presence:** Stay visible and active in relevant networks. Join professional organizations, participate in online forums, and engage in community activities related to your field.

> *Pro Tip:* Building relationships takes time and consistency. Regular, positive interactions are key to establishing trust and rapport.

Developing Trust

Trust is a critical component of any professional relationship. To build trust:

- **Be Reliable:** Follow through on your commitments and promises. Reliability builds credibility.
- **Share Information:** When appropriate, offer valuable insights and information. Sharing knowledge can establish you as a trusted resource.
- **Respect Confidentiality:** Maintain confidentiality and discretion when handling sensitive information. Respect for privacy fosters trust.

> **Pro Tip:** Trust is earned over time through consistent and ethical behavior. Always prioritize integrity in your interactions.

Maintaining Professionalism

- **Balancing Competition and Cooperation:** The legislative arena is inherently competitive, but maintaining professionalism is crucial. Here are some strategies for balancing competition and cooperation:
- **Recognize Shared Goals:** Identify areas where your interests align with those of other lobbyists. Focus on common goals rather than differences.
- **Respect Differences:** Acknowledge that not all lobbyists will share your perspective. Respect differing viewpoints and seek to understand their rationale.
- **Avoid Personal Conflicts:** Keep interactions professional and avoid letting personal conflicts interfere with your work. Address disagreements calmly and constructively.

Pro Tip: Professionalism enhances your reputation and facilitates productive collaborations. Approach every interaction with a focus on mutual respect and understanding. There have been times when I have had to work with someone I truly disliked. I was not too fond of their style or behaviors; everything about them went against my grain. But in the end, I had to get over it and work with them. It was a tough row to hoe, but I managed it, and we passed the bill.

Effective Communication

Clear and effective communication is essential for building and maintaining relationships. Consider the following tips:

- **Be Clear and Concise:** Communicate your points clearly and concisely, avoid jargon, and ensure your message is easily understood.

- **Listen Actively:** Practice active listening by paying full attention to the speaker, acknowledging their points, and responding thoughtfully.

- **Be Transparent:** Maintain transparency in your interactions. Honesty and openness build trust and credibility.

Pro Tip: Effective communication involves both speaking and listening. Strive for a balance that fosters mutual understanding and respect.

Section 4: Strategic Collaboration

Strategic collaboration is a powerful tool in the legislative arena, allowing lobbyists to amplify their influence, pool resources, and achieve common goals more effectively. This section guides forming coalitions, sharing resources, and leveraging collective strengths for successful advocacy.

Forming Coalitions

- **Identify Potential Partners:** The first step in forming a successful coalition is identifying potential partners who share your interests and goals. Look for organizations and lobbyists with complementary strengths and a track record of effective advocacy in areas that align with your objectives.

Pro Tip: Start by mapping out the landscape of stakeholders in your field. Consider reaching out to those with whom you have previously worked successfully or who have demonstrated a commitment to similar causes.

- **Define Common Goals:** Once you have identified potential partners, clearly defining the coalition's common goals is crucial. Ensure that all members are aligned and committed to these objectives. This clarity will help keep the coalition focused and effective.

Pro Tip: Successful coalitions often have a specific, well-defined mission that unites their members. Be specific about what you aim to achieve and how you plan to achieve it.

- **Establish Roles and Responsibilities:** Define each coalition member's roles and responsibilities to ensure efficient collaboration. This includes assigning tasks, setting deadlines, and establishing mechanisms for accountability. Clear role definitions help prevent misunderstandings and ensure that all members contribute effectively.

> **Pro Tip:** Create a formal agreement or memorandum of understanding (MOU) outlining each member's roles, responsibilities, and expectations. This document can serve as a reference and help maintain accountability.

- **Communicate Regularly:** Regular communication is essential for maintaining a cohesive and effective coalition. Schedule regular meetings, update members on progress, and address any issues promptly. Consistent communication keeps everyone informed and engaged.

> **Pro Tip:** Use a variety of communication channels, such as email, video conferences, and in-person meetings, to ensure that all members stay connected and informed.

Sharing Resources

- **Leverage Expertise:** One of the primary benefits of forming a coalition is the ability to leverage the expertise of its members. Each member brings unique skills, knowledge, and perspectives that can enhance the coalition's efforts.

> **Pro Tip:** Encourage members to share their expertise through workshops, training sessions, and collaborative research projects. This collective knowledge can significantly strengthen your advocacy efforts.

- **Combine Data and Research:** Pooling research and data from multiple sources can create a comprehensive and compelling case for your advocacy. Share relevant studies, reports, and data sets with coalition members to build a robust evidence base.

Pro Tip: Collaborative research projects can also enhance the credibility and impact of your advocacy. Consider commissioning joint studies or surveys to gather data that supports your coalition's goals.

- **Coordinate Efforts:** Coordinating activities within the coalition can maximize impact and avoid duplication of efforts. Develop a shared action plan that outlines key activities, timelines, and milestones. This coordination ensures that all members are cohesively working towards the same objectives.

Pro Tip: Use project management tools and platforms to keep track of activities, deadlines, and responsibilities. This can help streamline coordination and ensure that everyone stays on track.

Leveraging Collective Strengths

- **Amplify Your Voice:** A well-organized coalition can amplify your voice and increase your influence on key issues. By presenting a united front, you can demonstrate broad support for your cause and enhance your credibility with legislators and other stakeholders.

Pro Tip: Joint press releases, public statements, and coordinated advocacy campaigns can help amplify your message and draw more attention to your cause.

- **Maximize Impact:** Strategic collaboration allows you to maximize the impact of your advocacy efforts. By pooling resources, expertise, and networks, you can achieve greater reach and effectiveness than working alone.

> **Pro Tip:** Regularly assess the impact of your coalition's efforts and adjust your strategies as needed. Use metrics and feedback to measure progress and identify areas for improvement.

- **Enhance Credibility:** Working with diverse stakeholders can enhance your credibility and demonstrate broad-based support for your cause. This can be particularly persuasive to legislators and policymakers, who are often influenced by the level of public and stakeholder support.

> **Pro Tip:** Highlight the diversity and expertise of your coalition members in your communications and advocacy materials. This can help strengthen your case and build trust with your audience.

By mastering the art of strategic collaboration, you can harness your coalition's collective strengths, amplify your influence, and achieve your advocacy goals more effectively. Focus on forming strong coalitions, sharing resources, and leveraging collective strengths to navigate the legislative arena with confidence and success.

Section 5: Communication Skills

Effective communication is at the heart of successful lobbying. It is essential for building relationships, persuading stakeholders, and advancing your objectives. This section explores key strategies for clear and persuasive communication and techniques for resolving conflicts and finding common ground.

Effective Communication

Be Clear and Concise: Clear and concise communication is vital in the legislative arena, where time is often limited, and attention spans can be short. Here are some tips to enhance clarity and conciseness:

- **Define Your Message:** Know what you want to communicate and stay focused on that message. Avoid unnecessary details that can dilute your point.
- **Use Simple Language:** Avoid jargon and technical terms that may not be familiar to all your audience. Use straightforward language that is easy to understand.
- **Structure Your Information:** Organize your message logically, with a clear beginning, middle, and end. This helps your audience follow your argument and retain key points.

> *Pro Tip:* Practice summarizing your message in a few sentences. This exercise helps you distill your main points and communicate more effectively.

Listen Actively: Active listening is crucial for understanding others and building rapport. It involves fully concentrating on the speaker's words, understanding their message, and responding thoughtfully. Here are some strategies for active listening:

- **Pay Attention:** Give the speaker your full attention. Avoid distractions and focus on their words, tone, and body language.
- **Show That You're Listening:** Use verbal and non-verbal cues, such as nodding, maintaining eye contact, and providing feedback like "I see" or "I understand."

- **Reflect and Clarify:** Paraphrase the speaker's message to ensure you understand correctly. Ask clarifying questions if needed.

> *Pro Tip:* Active listening builds trust and demonstrates respect. It can also provide valuable insights into the speaker's perspective and needs.

Be Persuasive: Persuasive communication is essential for influencing legislators and other stakeholders. Here are some techniques to enhance your persuasiveness:

- **Use Evidence:** Support your arguments with data, research, and real-world examples. This adds credibility and weight to your message.
- **Tell Stories:** Use storytelling to make your message more relatable and memorable. Personal stories and anecdotes can humanize your arguments and engage your audience emotionally.
- **Address Counterarguments:** Anticipate and address potential objections to your message. This demonstrates thoroughness and prepares you for pushback.

> *Pro Tip:* Practice your persuasive techniques through role-playing and feedback sessions. This helps refine your skills and build confidence.

Section 6: Conflict Resolution

Recognize Conflict: Conflict is inevitable in the legislative arena, given the diverse interests and high stakes involved. Recognizing the signs of conflict early can help you address it before it escalates. Look for:

- **Disagreements:** Frequent or intense disagreements on key issues.

- **Tension:** Increased tension or hostility in interactions.

- **Communication Breakdown:** Reduced or strained communication between parties.

Pro Tip: Early recognition of conflict allows for timely intervention and resolution. Addressing issues proactively can prevent escalation and foster more productive relationships.

Address Conflict Constructively: When conflict arises, addressing it constructively is crucial for maintaining professionalism and finding common ground. Here are some strategies:

- **Stay Calm:** Approach the situation calmly and avoid reacting emotionally. This helps keep the conversation productive and focused on resolution.

- **Focus on Issues, Not Personalities:** Address the specific issues at hand rather than attacking or blaming individuals. This keeps the discussion objective and solution oriented.

- **Seek to Understand:** Try to understand the other party's perspective and needs. This can reveal underlying interests and potential areas for compromise.

Pro Tip: Use "I" statements to express your concerns and needs without blaming others. For example, "I feel concerned when deadlines are missed" rather than "You never meet deadlines."

Find Common Ground: Finding common ground is key to resolving conflicts and advancing collaborative efforts. Here are some techniques:

- **Identify Shared Interests:** Look for areas where your interests align with those of the other party. Focus on these common goals to build a foundation for cooperation.

- **Explore Options Together:** Brainstorm potential solutions collaboratively. This can generate creative ideas and foster a sense of joint ownership over the resolution.

- **Be Willing to Compromise:** Recognize that compromise may be necessary to reach a mutually acceptable solution. Be flexible and open to adjusting your position.

> **Pro Tip:** Effective conflict resolution can strengthen relationships and build trust. Handling conflicts with professionalism and respect demonstrates your commitment to constructive collaboration.

Mastering effective communication and conflict resolution skills, enhance your ability to build relationships, persuade stakeholders, and navigate the legislative arena successfully. Focus on clarity, active listening, persuasiveness, and constructive conflict resolution to achieve your advocacy goals and foster productive collaborations.

Section 7: Handling Irreconcilable Differences

Not all relationships in the legislature will be harmonious. Sometimes, lobbyist differences can be so significant that collaboration is not feasible. Handling these irreconcilable differences with professionalism and strategic acumen is essential to maintaining your effectiveness and reputation. This section guides recognizing when collaboration isn't possible, alternative strategies for working around these challenges, and maintaining professionalism despite the conflict.

Recognizing the Signs

When Collaboration Isn't Possible: It's important to recognize the signs that collaboration with another lobbyist is not feasible. Some indicators include:

- **Consistent Conflicts:** Repeated and unresolved disagreements on key issues.
- **Lack of Trust:** A history of broken promises or unethical behavior that undermines trust.
- **Opposing Goals:** Fundamental differences in objectives that cannot be reconciled.

> *Pro Tip:* Be honest about the feasibility of working with certain individuals. If past attempts at collaboration have consistently failed, it might be time to consider alternative approaches.

Evaluating Impact

Assess the impact of these irreconcilable differences on your overall strategy. Determine whether the conflict significantly hinders your ability to achieve your goals or if it can be managed without major disruptions.

> *Pro Tip:* Not every conflict will substantially impact your objectives. Sometimes, it's possible to work around the issue without significant consequences.

Alternative Strategies

Indirect Collaboration: When direct collaboration isn't possible, consider indirect collaboration through mutual contacts or intermediaries.

Working with trusted third parties who can mediate or represent your interests can help bridge the gap.

> **Pro Tip:** Identify individuals or organizations with good relationships with both parties and can serve as neutral intermediaries. This can facilitate communication and collaboration without direct interaction.

Parallel Efforts: In some cases, pursuing parallel efforts may be the best approach. This involves working independently towards your goals while avoiding direct conflict with the other lobbyist's efforts.

Strategies for Parallel Efforts:

- **Separate Focus:** Concentrate on different aspects of the issue where your efforts do not overlap.

- **Independent Advocacy:** Develop independent advocacy campaigns that do not directly conflict with those of the opposing lobbyist.

- **Coexistence:** Acknowledge the existence of differing approaches and work to coexist without direct interference.

> **Pro Tip:** Parallel efforts require careful coordination to ensure that your activities do not inadvertently undermine each other. To avoid conflicts, regularly assess the impact of both efforts.

- **Strategic Alliances:** Forming new alliances with other lobbyists or organizations can help counterbalance the influence of uncooperative lobbyists. These strategic alliances can provide additional support and resources to advance your objectives.

> **Pro Tip:** Look for potential allies who share your goals and are affected by the uncooperative lobbyist's actions. Building a strong coalition can enhance your collective influence.

Maintaining Professionalism

Ensuring Professionalism: Maintaining professionalism is crucial even when conflicts arise. Your reputation and effectiveness depend on your ability to handle difficult situations gracefully and with integrity.

Guidelines for Maintaining Professionalism:

- **Stay Focused on Issues:** Discuss policy and issues rather than personal grievances.

- **Avoid Public Disputes:** Avoid engaging in public conflicts or disparaging remarks. These can damage your reputation and undermine your credibility.

- **Demonstrate Respect:** Respect the other lobbyist's views, even if you strongly disagree. Professional courtesy fosters a positive working environment.

> **Pro Tip:** Professionalism in the face of conflict can enhance your reputation and build trust with legislators and other stakeholders. It demonstrates your commitment to constructive advocacy and ethical conduct.

Managing Emotional Responses: Conflicts can be emotionally charged, but managing your emotional responses is essential to maintain professionalism. Here are some strategies:

- **Take a Step Back:** If a situation becomes too heated, take a break to cool down and gain perspective.

- **Seek Support:** Talk to trusted colleagues or mentors for advice and support. They can provide valuable insights and help you navigate conflict.

- **Focus on Long-Term Goals:** Keep your long-term objectives in mind and avoid getting bogged down by short-term conflicts.

> **Pro Tip:** Emotional intelligence is key to managing conflicts effectively. Practice self-awareness and self-regulation to handle difficult situations with composure.

You can navigate irreconcilable differences by recognizing when collaboration isn't possible, adopting alternative strategies, and maintaining professionalism. These skills will help you preserve your reputation, achieve your advocacy goals, and maintain positive relationships in the legislative arena.

Thriving Through Collaboration

Navigating the legislative arena requires a strategic approach to building and maintaining relationships with fellow lobbyists. I explored the essential elements of collaboration, from understanding the diverse types of lobbyists to mastering effective communication and conflict resolution. We've also addressed the challenging scenarios where collaboration isn't feasible, offering alternative strategies to ensure you remain effective and professional.

Building solid relationships with other lobbyists is not just about advancing your goals; it's about being able to work with all kinds of people to obtain your client's goals and have a work environment that works for everyone,

"Elected officials are like weather forecasters—they can be wrong most of the time and still keep their jobs."

— Unknown

Chapter 17: Investing in Influence

"Lobbying at the state level can be a significant expense, with well-funded interest groups spending large sums to influence legislation. This creates a financial barrier for smaller organizations and individuals who may struggle to have their voices heard."

— *Jessica A. Levinson*

Engaging in political activities through lobbying and advocacy is critical for any organization aiming to influence public policy. However, lobbying and advocacy have substantial and multifaceted costs. Understanding these costs is essential for budgeting and ensuring a successful lobbying campaign.

Your political program has direct and indirect expenses associated with it. Direct expenses include the fees paid to professional lobbyists, which vary widely and are based on expertise, reputation, and the complexity of the legislative issue. These fees are often structured as monthly retainers, hourly rates, or success fees contingent on achieving specific outcomes.

While direct expenses are the most visible, indirect expenses play a crucial role in a comprehensive lobbying effort. These include research and data collection, travel and accommodation, hosting events, and communication efforts. Compliance with legal and regulatory requirements is also a significant indirect cost. By considering all these aspects, organizations can ensure they are fully prepared for the complexities of the political process.

Moreover, the complexity of the legislative issue significantly impacts the overall budget. Broad, multi-faceted issues with widespread implications require more extensive resources and longer-term commitments than narrowly focused, localized issues. The number and diversity of stakeholders involved, the regulatory environment, and the geographic scope of the campaign all contribute to the complexity and consequently the cost.

In the following sections, we will break down the typical fee structures for lobbyists, identify the hidden costs that can arise during a lobbying effort, and provide real-world examples of how different factors influence the budget. Additionally, I offer tools and strategies for calculating the return on investment (ROI) of lobbying activities, helping you to make the most of your investment in legislative advocacy.

In this chapter you will learn about

- Understanding the costs.
- The types of lobbyist services.
- How to calculate ROI.
- Real world examples.
- Complex issues.
- Negotiating the fees.

- Legal and compliance *considerations.*

Section 1: Understanding the Costs

Factors Influencing Costs

The cost of hiring a professional lobbyist can vary significantly based on several factors. Understanding these factors can help you make an informed decision.

- **Expertise and Reputation:** Highly experienced and reputable lobbyists typically command higher fees. Their deep understanding of the legislative process and established relationships with key stakeholders can significantly enhance their effectiveness.
- **Geographic Location:** Lobbying costs can vary by region. For example, hiring a lobbyist in Washington, DC, where federal lobbying is concentrated, may be more expensive than hiring one in a smaller state capital.
- **Scope of Work:** The complexity and breadth of the lobbying effort also influence costs. A comprehensive campaign that includes strategy development, direct lobbying, public relations, and coalition building will cost more than a focused effort on a single issue.

> **Pro Tip:** Clearly define the scope of work and objectives from the outset. This helps set a realistic budget and ensures you get the most value from your investment.

Typical Fee Structures

Lobbyists typically offer their services through various fee structures. Understanding these structures can help you choose the best option for your needs.

- **Retainer Fees:** Many lobbyists work on a retainer basis, charging a fixed monthly fee for their services. This arrangement provides consistent support and is often used for long-term lobbying efforts.
- **Hourly Rates:** Some lobbyists charge by the hour. This fee structure is common for short-term projects or when specific tasks require intensive effort over a short period.
- **Success Fees:** Success fees are contingent upon achieving specific outcomes, such as passing a bill or securing funding. This structure aligns the lobbyist's incentives with your goals but can be more expensive if the target is met. <u>**Check your state lobbying laws regarding success fees, In most states this kind of payment is illegal.**</u>

Section 2: Types of Lobbyist Services

Lobbyists offer various services tailored to meet the needs of their clients. The type of service required depends on the lobbying effort's specific goals, the legislative issue's complexity, and the resources available. Understanding three of the different types of lobbyist services can help organizations choose the right approach for their advocacy efforts.

1. Comprehensive Services

Full-Service Lobbying

Description: Full-service lobbying firms provide a wide range of services, encompassing all aspects of a lobbying campaign. These firms manage everything from strategy development to implementation and evaluation.

Components:

- **Strategic Planning:** Developing a comprehensive strategy that outlines the goals, target legislators, key messages, and tactics.

- **Direct Lobbying:** Engaging directly with legislators and their staff to advocate for the client's position. This includes arranging meetings, providing testimony at hearings, and building relationships.

- **Coalition Building:** Forming and managing coalitions with other organizations to amplify the advocacy effort.

- **Public Relations and Media Outreach:** Crafting and disseminating press releases, managing media relations, and developing communication materials to influence public opinion.

- **Research and Analysis:** Conducting detailed policy research and analysis to support the lobbying effort with data-driven arguments.

- **Event Management:** Organizing events such as briefings, receptions, and conferences to raise awareness and build support.

Example: A healthcare reform campaign that involves nationwide advocacy, media engagement, and coalition building across multiple sectors would benefit from full-service lobbying.

2. Specialized Services

Issue-Specific Advocacy

Description: Specialized lobbying focused on a particular issue or set of issues. This type of service is ideal for organizations with a narrow focus or specific legislative goals.

Components:

- **Targeted Strategy:** Developing a focused strategy that addresses the specific issue.
- **Legislative Monitoring:** Keeping track of relevant legislative developments and informing the client about critical updates.
- **Expert Testimony:** Providing expert witnesses to testify at legislative hearings or regulatory meetings.
- **Stakeholder Engagement:** Engaging with specific stakeholders directly affected by the issue.

Example: An environmental organization seeking to pass a specific clean water regulation might engage a lobbyist specializing in environmental policy.

Regulatory Compliance and Advisory

Description: Services aimed at helping clients navigate complex regulatory environments. This is crucial for industries heavily impacted by regulations, such as finance, healthcare, and energy.

Components:

- **Regulatory Analysis:** Assessing current and proposed regulations to understand their impact on the client's operations.

- **Compliance Support:** Assisting with compliance efforts to ensure the client meets all regulatory requirements.
- **Advocacy for Regulatory Change:** Lobbying for changes to existing unfavorable regulations for the client.

Example: A financial institution might hire a lobbyist to navigate new banking regulations and advocate for favorable adjustments.

Crisis Management

Description: Specialized services to handle legislative or regulatory crises that require immediate and strategic intervention.

Components:

- **Rapid Response:** Quickly developing and implementing a response strategy to address the crisis.
- **Legislative Defense:** Engaging with legislators to mitigate or reverse adverse legislative actions.
- **Public Relations:** Managing the public narrative through media outreach and communication strategies.

Example: A company facing sudden regulatory action that threatens its operations might need a crisis management lobbyist to intervene and protect its interests.

3. Ad Hoc and Project-Based Services

Short-Term Projects

Description: Lobbying services for specific, time-limited projects. This is suitable for organizations that do not require ongoing lobbying support but need help with a particular legislative effort.

Components:

- **Project Planning:** Developing a detailed plan for the project, including timelines, objectives, and key actions.
- **Implementation:** Executing the project plan, which may include lobbying efforts, stakeholder engagement, and media outreach.
- **Evaluation:** Assessing the project's outcomes and reporting the results.

Example: An industry group might hire a lobbyist for a short-term campaign to secure funding for a new infrastructure project.

The type of lobbyist service required depends on the organization's goals, the complexity of the issue, and the resources available. Comprehensive services offer a full range of support for large-scale campaigns, while specialized services provide targeted expertise for specific issues or regulatory challenges. Ad hoc and project-based services offer flexibility for short-term or narrowly focused efforts. Organizations can make informed decisions that align with their strategic objectives and budget constraints by understanding the different types of lobbyist services.

Section 3: Calculating ROI

Return on investment (ROI) in lobbying is not always easy to measure, but it is crucial for understanding the value of your investment. ROI can be defined in various ways, depending on your objectives.

- **Legislative Success:** The most direct measure of ROI is the successful passage of legislation or regulatory changes that benefit your organization.
- **Cost Savings:** Achieving regulatory relief or preventing unfavorable legislation can result in significant cost savings.
- **Market Opportunities:** Lobbying can open up new market opportunities by shaping policies that create favorable conditions for your business.

> **Pro Tip:** Define your objectives clearly at the outset. This will help you set measurable goals and track the success of your lobbying efforts.

Key Performance Indicators

Identify key performance indicators (KPIs) that align with your objectives to measure ROI effectively. Common KPIs include:

- **Legislative Wins:** Number of bills passed or defeated that align with your goals.
- **Cost Avoidance:** Savings achieved by preventing unfavorable legislation or regulations.
- **Policy Influence:** The extent to which your lobbying efforts have influenced policy debates and decisions.
- **Stakeholder Engagement:** Levels of engagement and support from key stakeholders and policymakers.

> **Pro Tip:** Review these KPIs regularly to assess the effectiveness of your lobbying efforts. Adjust your strategies as needed to maximize ROI.

Section 4: Real-World Examples

Case Studies

Real-world examples can provide valuable insights into the ROI of lobbying efforts. Here are two illustrative case studies:

1. Construction Industry Advocacy

- **Objective:** To change the contract law that reduced subcontractor exposure to liability in construction defects.
- **Strategy:** The lobbying firm developed a comprehensive strategy that included direct lobbying, public relations, and coalition building with other subcontractor organizations.
- **Outcome:** The initiative reduced insurance premiums and legal costs for subcontractors and clearly defined subcontractor liability in construction defects cases, far exceeding the $75,000 lobbying budget. The ROI in terms of direct financial return was twenty-five times the investment.

2. Electrical Apprentice Manpower Advocacy

- **Objective:** To change the apprentice ratio for electricians.
- **Strategy:** The lobbying firm focused on building relationships with key legislators, providing expert testimony, and mobilizing grassroots support.
- **Outcome:** The statute changed the apprentice ratio from one journeyman to one master electrician to three journeymen to

one master electrician, giving greater management control of staffing. With a lobbying expenditure of $45,000, the ROI on staffing costs was fifteen times the investment.

Lessons Learned

- **Strategic Alignment:** Aligning lobbying efforts with broader organizational goals enhances the chances of success.
- **Effective Communication:** Clear and persuasive communication with stakeholders and policymakers is crucial.
- **Adaptability:** The key to maintaining momentum and achieving objectives is adapting strategies in response to changing political dynamics.

Determining the ROI of lobbying services is critical for both lobbyists and their clients. From a lobbyist's perspective, ROI goes beyond just passing or defeating a piece of legislation. It's about demonstrating the tangible value your efforts bring to a client's goals. To start, it's important to clearly understand the client's objectives and align them with realistic outcomes. Are they looking to pass specific legislation, prevent harmful bills, or build long-term relationships with policymakers? Defining these goals upfront allows you to track progress and measure success against what matters most to the client. For instance, if stopping a harmful bill saves a client millions in compliance costs, or passing legislation creates new opportunities for growth, the ROI is both measurable and meaningful.

To calculate and present ROI, lobbyists must also evaluate the broader impact of their services. This includes factoring in cost savings, new revenue opportunities, and strengthened industry positioning that result from legislative wins. Additionally, soft returns, like improving a client's access to key decision-makers or raising their profile among lawmakers, are invaluable. As a lobbyist, being transparent about costs, regularly reporting on progress, and showing how each action supports the client's bottom line are essential to demonstrating value. Ultimately, ROI isn't just about dollars—it's about making strategic investments that deliver measurable benefits, solve problems, and create long-term success in the legislative arena. A client who sees the connection between your efforts and their outcomes will view your services not as a cost but as a critical investment.

Section 5: The Complexity of the Issues Dictates the Impact on Budgets

The complexity of the legislative issue significantly influences the budget required for a successful lobbying effort. Several factors contribute to this complexity, each of which can drive up costs differently. Here's a detailed explanation of how complexity affects the budget.

1. Scope of the Issue

Broad vs. Narrow Focus:

- **Broad Issues:** Issues that affect multiple sectors or have widespread implications typically require more extensive research, broader coalition-building efforts, and more sustained lobbying campaigns. For instance, lobbying for a national healthcare reform initiative would be more complex and costly than lobbying for a specific local environmental regulation.

- **Narrow Issues:** Targeted issues with a limited scope might require fewer extensive resources. For example, advocating for a specific tax benefit for a niche industry could be more straightforward and less costly.

Example: Lobbying for comprehensive climate change legislation involves addressing various sectors (energy, transportation, agriculture), whereas lobbying for a single renewable energy tax credit is more narrowly focused.

2. Stakeholder Involvement

Number and Diversity of Stakeholders:

- **High Stakeholder Engagement:** Complex issues often involve multiple stakeholders, including government agencies, industry groups, non-profits, and public interest groups. Managing these relationships and building consensus requires more time, effort, and resources.
- **Low Stakeholder Engagement:** Issues with fewer stakeholders or more homogeneous groups are generally easier and less expensive to manage.

Example: A campaign to reform the entire healthcare system involves numerous stakeholders (hospitals, insurance companies, patients, pharmaceutical companies), compared to a campaign focused on a single policy affecting a specific group, like the state practice act for Podiatrists.

3. Regulatory and Legislative Environment

Level of Regulatory and Legislative Complexity:

- **Highly Regulated Areas:** Issues in highly regulated areas like finance, healthcare, and environmental protection require deep expertise, ongoing compliance monitoring, and, often, the engagement of specialized legal and regulatory consultants. This drives up costs.

- **Less Regulated Areas:** Lobbying in areas with less regulatory oversight may be simpler and less expensive.

4. Geographic Scope

Local vs. National vs. International Issues:

- **National and International Scope:** Issues that span multiple states or countries require coordination across different jurisdictions, each with its own legislative and regulatory environment. This increases complexity and costs.
- **Local Scope:** Local issues, while potentially complex, generally involve fewer jurisdictions and are thus less costly to manage.

Example: Lobbying for federal data privacy legislation requires addressing national policies and potential international implications, compared to lobbying for a city ordinance on local business regulations.

5. Duration of the Campaign

Short-term vs. Long-term Efforts:

- **Long-term Campaigns:** Complex issues often necessitate prolonged lobbying efforts. Over months or years, sustained engagement increases costs related to staffing, research, and ongoing advocacy activities.
- **Short-term Campaigns:** Issues that can be addressed with a shorter, more intensive effort may incur fewer overall costs.

Example: A multi-year campaign to overhaul homelessness policy will require a significantly larger budget than a short-term push to pass workers' compensation reform.

6. Required Expertise

Specialized vs. General Expertise:

- **Specialized Expertise:** Complex issues often require lobbyists with specialized knowledge or experience. This expertise comes at a premium, as these professionals command higher fees.
- **General Expertise:** Issues that can be managed with general lobbying expertise may be less costly.

Example: Lobbying for advanced technological regulations in AI requires specialized technical and legal expertise, whereas lobbyists with broader expertise might manage general business regulation changes.

The complexity of a legislative issue significantly impacts the budget required for effective lobbying. Factors such as the scope of the issue, stakeholder involvement, regulatory environment, geographic scope, campaign duration, and required expertise all contribute to the overall cost. By understanding these factors, organizations can better plan and allocate resources to maximize their return on investment in lobbying efforts.

Section 6: Negotiating the Fees

Everything is negotiable! Nothing is off the table. Negotiating the costs associated with getting your lobbying fee, and developing agency budget involves several strategic steps. These steps ensure you get what you are worth, while maintaining the quality and effectiveness of your lobbying efforts. Here's a detailed guide on how to negotiate these costs effectively.

1. Understand the Market Rates

Before entering negotiations, research the average market rates for lobbying services in your area. This includes understanding the typical retainer fees, hourly rates, success fees, and other related costs. A clear idea of these rates helps you set realistic expectations and identify whether the proposed fee is reasonable.

Sources for Market Rates:

- Industry reports and surveys
- Professional associations such as the American League of Lobbyists
- Peers and industry insiders
- Lobbyists' reports filed with the state regulatory agency

2. Define Clear Objectives and Scope

Clearly defining your lobbying effort's scope of work and objectives is crucial. This includes specifying the issues to be addressed, the expected outcomes, and the campaign duration. A well-defined scope helps prevent scope creep, which can lead to increased costs.

Pro Tip:
- Outline specific goals and milestones.
- Identify key deliverables and timelines.
- Agree on the level of engagement required from the lobbyist.

3. Provide Detailed Proposals

When offering lobbying services, provide a detailed proposal. It should include a breakdown of costs, the scope of services provided, and the methodologies used.

Key Components of a Proposal:

- Detailed fee structure (retainer, hourly, success fees)
- Breakdown of additional costs (research, travel, event hosting)
- Description of services and deliverables
- Timelines and milestones

4. Negotiate Your Terms and Fees

You can begin negotiating terms and fees with knowledge of market rates and detailed proposals. Here are some strategies for effective negotiation:

Retainer Fees

- **Flexibility:** Ask if the retainer fee can be adjusted based on the complexity and scope of your campaign.
- **Incremental Payments:** Propose spreading the retainer fee for the campaign rather than all upfront.

Hourly Rates

- **Volume Discount:** Negotiate for discounted hourly rates if a significant number of required hours.
- **Cap on Hours:** Set a cap on the number of billable hours per month to control costs.

Additional Costs

- **Travel and Accommodation:** Negotiate travel and accommodation expenses, possibly limiting these costs or requiring approval for trips beyond a certain distance.

- **Event Hosting and PR:** Request detailed budgets for events and public relations activities and look for opportunities to cut unnecessary expenses.

5. Consider Long-Term Relationships

Building a long-term relationship with a client can provide benefits such as loyalty discounts and better service due to the firm's deeper understanding of the client's needs. Discuss potential long-term collaboration during negotiations and inquire about any discounts or benefits that may come with a long-term contract.

6. Regular Review and Adjustment

Agree on regular reviews of the lobbying campaign to assess progress and costs. This allows you to adjust the budget and scope as needed and ensures you get value for your money.

> **Pro Tips:** for Regular Review:
> - Schedule quarterly reviews.
> - Assess progress against milestones.
> - Adjust strategies and budgets based on current performance and changing needs.

7. Legal and Compliance Considerations

Ensure that all negotiated terms comply with legal and ethical standards for lobbying. If necessary, consult legal experts to review contracts and agreements.

Compliance Tips

- Ensure transparency in reporting and billing.
- Adhere to all lobbying disclosure requirements.

- Maintain ethical standards in all lobbying activities.

Negotiating the costs of developing a legislative budget requires thorough research, clear communication, and strategic planning. By understanding market rates, defining the scope of work, comparing proposals, and negotiating terms, you can effectively manage your lobbying expenses and maximize the return on your investment. Regular reviews and compliance with legal standards further ensure the success and integrity of your lobbying efforts.

Final Thoughts

Engaging in the political process through lobbying and advocacy is essential for any organization aiming to influence public policy. However, it comes with substantial costs that must be carefully managed to ensure success. Understanding these costs and negotiating effectively can help organizations maximize their return on investment and achieve their legislative goals.

By thoroughly understanding the landscape of lobbying costs, the lobbyist and the organizations can make informed decisions about their investments in political involvement with each other. Effective negotiation, regular reviews, and adherence to legal and ethical standards are crucial for ensuring the success and integrity of lobbying efforts.

As you move forward, use the insights and strategies outlined in this chapter to navigate the financial aspects of lobbying confidently. Remember, the key to successful political involvement lies in careful planning, strategic investment, and continuous evaluation of your efforts. Mastering these elements allows you to engage effectively in the legislative process, achieve your advocacy goals, and make a meaningful impact on public policy.

Every profession or trade has its own set of unique tools. Professional lobbyists have their toolbox containing these tools. All are designed to help them develop plans and strategies to obtain their clients' goals. This next chapter will explain them in detail.

"I don't make jokes. I just watch the government and
report the facts."

— Will Rogers

Chapter 18: **What is in Your Toolbox**

"Effective lobbying means using every tool available — from direct lobbying to grassroots mobilization, media campaigns, coalition-building, and research reports — to shape opinion and influence legislative outcomes. It's not just about access; it's about creating the perception of broad support for your issue."

— *Lee Drutman*

As a lobbyist, I've learned that having the right tools can make all the difference between success and frustration in navigating the legislative process. Over the years, I've built a "toolbox" of resources and strategies that I rely on daily to represent my clients effectively. These tools range from bill tracking systems that keep me updated on legislative developments to relationship management techniques that help me stay connected with key legislators and stakeholders. One of the most indispensable tools in my kit is a reliable legislative calendar. It may seem simple but knowing every critical deadline, hearing date, and floor session ensures I'm always ahead of the game.

Early in my career, I once missed an important committee meeting because I didn't have a centralized system for tracking events, and I vowed never to let that happen again. Now, I ensure every detail is accounted for, giving me confidence and precision in my work.

Another essential tool is a clear communication strategy, which includes everything from crafting compelling talking points to effectively using technology and media platforms. For instance, I've used targeted email campaigns and social media to rally grassroots support for a bill, giving legislators a tangible sense of public interest. I've also leveraged relationship-building tools, like stakeholder mapping, to identify and engage key allies who can help move a bill forward. Of course, every tool has its advantages and limitations—what works for one situation might not work for another, so adaptability is key. In this chapter, I share seventeen essential tools I've used throughout my career, along with tips for making the most of them. Whether you're drafting legislation, lobbying a tough committee, or mobilizing support, these tools will prepare you to tackle any challenge the legislative process throws your way.

Key Points

- Identifying the tools of the trade
- How are they used to obtain the desired results

1. Key Contact Program

A key contact program connects lobbyists and their clients with influential individuals with strong relationships with legislators.

Pros:

- **Direct Access:** Facilitates direct communication with key decision-makers.
- **Influence:** Leverages established relationships to sway opinions and votes.

Cons:

- **Time-Consuming:** Building and maintaining these relationships takes considerable time and effort.
- **Dependency:** Heavy reliance on a few key contacts can be risky if those individuals lose influence.
- **Benefits:** Utilizing a key contact program ensures your messages reach the right ears, increasing the likelihood of favorable legislative outcomes.

> *Pro Tip:* Always diversify your contacts to avoid over-reliance on a single individual. It's like having multiple can openers—you never know when one might jam.

2. Grassroots Program

A grassroots program mobilizes many individuals to advocate for a cause, creating a groundswell of support.

Pros:

- **Broad Support:** Engages a wide base of advocates.
- **Visibility:** Increases issue visibility through widespread public support.

Cons:

- **Coordination:** Requires significant coordination and communication.
- **Control:** When many voices are involved, it is harder to control the message.
- **Benefits:** Grassroots Programs can create a powerful, effective force that pressures legislators to favor your client's interests.

> **Pro Tip:** Use humor and relatable content to engage your grassroots base. Consider adding a spoonful of sugar to help the medicine go down.

3. Legislative Tracking Service

A legislative tracking service monitors and reports on legislative activities, including bill progress and critical votes.

Pros:

- **Timeliness:** Provides real-time updates on legislative activities.
- **Comprehensive:** Covers a wide range of legislative actions.

Cons:

- **Cost:** High-quality services can be expensive.
- **Overload:** This may produce information overload if not appropriately managed.
- **Benefits:** With legislative tracking services, you stay informed and proactive, allowing you to respond quickly to legislative changes that impact your clients.

> **Pro Tip:** Use filters and set priorities within the tracking service to focus on the most relevant updates. It's like having a spam filter for your legislative inbox.

4. Coalition Building

Coalition building is forming alliances with other groups or organizations to strengthen advocacy efforts. Coalition Building can enhance your influence and resources, making your advocacy efforts more robust and impactful.

Pros:

- **Strength in Numbers:** Amplifies your voice through collective action.
- **Resource Sharing:** Shares the burden of costs and effort.

Cons:

- **Coordination:** Requires aligning goals and strategies, which can be challenging.
- **Compromise:** You may need to compromise on certain issues.
- **Leadership Struggles:** There can be leadership issues. Difficult to manage members.

> **Pro Tip:** Clear communication and defined roles are key. It's like running a relay race—everyone must know when to pass the baton.

5. Legislative Fact Sheets

These are concise, informative documents that provide legislators with crucial facts and arguments about your issue or a bill. Legislative fact sheets help convey your message effectively and efficiently, ensuring legislators understand your position quickly. They are a quick read, and legislators read them.

Pros:

- **Clarity:** Presents information clearly and succinctly.
- **Focus:** Keeps legislators focused on the most important points.

Cons:

- **Brevity:** Limited space can mean omitting important details to stress the importance of the legislation.
- **Distribution:** Ensuring they reach the right people can be a challenge.

> *Pro Tip:* Use bullet points and infographics. It's like dressing your argument in a snazzy suit—impossible to ignore.

6. Individual Legislator Profile

Detailed profiles of legislators, including their voting history, interests, family members and key issues allow you to tailor your advocacy strategies to resonate with each legislator's unique interests and concerns.

Pros:

- **Customization:** Tailors your approach based on specific legislator profiles.
- **Insight:** Provides deep insights into legislators' motivations and priorities.

Cons:

- **Maintenance:** Requires regular updates to stay current.
- **Depth:** Gathering detailed information can be time and labor-intensive. Building a legislator database requires constant updating to assure the information is current.

> **Pro Tip:** Think of these profiles as your secret weapon. Knowing a legislator's favorite coffee can be the key to a productive meeting.

7. Relationships with Legislative Staffer

Building relationships with the staff members who support legislators in handling their legislative responsibilities can provide valuable insights and access, enhancing your lobbying effectiveness. These are extremely important relationships that you need to build. Take care of staff and they will take care of you.

Pros:

- **Access:** Staffers often act as gatekeepers to legislators.
- **Influence:** Staffers can significantly influence a legislator's decisions.

- **Information:** Information resources for the activities of the legislator

Cons:

- **Turnover:** High staff turnover can disrupt established relationships.
- **Hierarchy:** Navigating staff hierarchies can be complex.

> *Pro Tip:* Always treat staffers with the same respect as legislators. Remember, they're the wizards behind the curtain.

8. Political Action Committees (PACs)

PACs are organizations that raise and spend money to elect or defeat political candidates or influence policy issues. They can amplify your political influence by supporting candidates championing your clients' causes.

Pros:

- **Influence:** Provides financial support to candidates who align with your interests.
- **Visibility:** Increases your visibility and influence in the political arena.

Cons:

- **Regulation:** Subject to stringent regulatory requirements.
- **Perception:** Can be perceived negatively by the public.

> **Pro Tip:** Ensure transparency and compliance. Failure to comply with regulations can turn your PAC into a political hot potato.

9. Get Out the Vote (GOTV) Campaigns

GOTV campaigns are efforts to encourage people to vote in elections. They can shape the political landscape by ensuring supportive voters turn out on election day.

Pros:

- Engagement: Mobilizes supporters to participate in the democratic process.
- Impact: Can significantly impact election outcomes.

Cons:

- Resource-Intensive: Requires substantial resources and coordination. Lots of human capital
- Effectiveness: Results can be unpredictable.

> **Pro Tip:** Use engaging and interactive content to motivate voters. Think of it as hosting a grand party—everyone needs a reason to show up.

10. Legislative Recognition

Legislative recognition programs, which recognize legislators for their support and legislative achievements, can build goodwill and motivate legislators to continue supporting their causes. This is one of my favorite tools to use with legislators. The good will that is created, and the strong relationship between you and the legislator is priceless. They will be your supporter forever.

Pros:

- **Motivation:** Encourages legislators to support your issues, builds relationships.
- **Positive Visibility:** Enhances your organization's public image.

Cons:

- **Perception:** May be viewed as insincere or self-serving.
- **Selection:** Selecting award recipients can be contentious.

> *Pro Tip:* Make the awards genuine and meaningful. Nobody likes a participation trophy, especially legislators.

11. Company Web Site

This may seem obvious to most people, but I can't tell you how many poorly constructed websites that did nothing for the image of the association. Spend the money and design an outstanding web site. Your website can serve as a central hub for your advocacy efforts, providing information and resources to clients and the public. It is the first impression that people receive when researching lobbying firms.

Pros:

- **Accessibility:** Provides 24/7 access to information.
- **Credibility:** Enhances your professional image and credibility.

- **Professionalism:** Demonstrates your professionalism to outsiders

Cons:

- **Maintenance:** Requires regular updates and maintenance.
- **Security:** Must ensure data security and privacy.
- **Expense:** It can be expensive to maintain

> **Pro Tip:** Keep the content fresh and engaging. Your website should be like a dynamic storefront window—always attracting attention.

12. Media Relationships

Effective media relations can amplify your message and reach a broader audience, influencing public opinion and legislative outcomes. A lot of associations do not have a budget for this. However, you as their lobbyist can connect them with the key reporters to get their message out to the public.

Pros:

- **Coverage:** Increases your issues' visibility through media coverage.
- **Credibility:** Media endorsements can enhance your credibility.

Cons:

- **Uncontrollable:** Media narratives can be unpredictable and uncontrollable.

- **Time-Consuming:** Building media relationships takes time and effort.

> **Pro Tip:** Develop a media kit with crucial information and visuals. Think of it as your story's sizzle reel.

13. Opposition Research

Opposition research equips you with the knowledge to counteract opposing efforts, strengthening your advocacy effectively. You must know your opposition. You must know them inside and out. You as the lobbyist know the players and can provide the information to your client. You can't fight something without knowing who the opposition is.

Pros:

- **Preparation:** Helps you anticipate and counter opposing arguments.
- **Strategy:** Informs your strategic planning.

Cons:

- **Ethical Concerns:** Must be conducted ethically to avoid negative repercussions.
- **Resource-Intensive:** Can require significant resources.

> **Pro Tip:** Always stay ethical. Think of it as playing chess, not poker—strategy over sleight of hand. Of course you will be ethical in your information gathering. You must know everything about the opposition. The better you know your opposition the greater your chances for coming out on top.

14. Strategic Legislative Plan

A strategic legislative plan is a roadmap for your advocacy efforts, helping you stay organized and focused on your objectives. Seriously, you can't do anything without a plan. You can't just go willy nilly with your campaign. You need a plan, so you know how to use your resources effectively to assure your desired outcome.

Pros:

- **Direction:** Provides clear direction and focus for your efforts.
- **Coordination:** Ensures all team members are aligned and working towards common goals.

Cons:

- **Flexibility:** You may need to adapt to changing circumstances.
- **Complexity:** Developing a thorough plan can be complex.

> **Pro Tip:** Review and update the plan regularly. It's like updating your GPS—new routes may lead to your destination faster.

15. Fundraising for Legislators

Fundraising for legislators can solidify your relationships and ensure you have allies in key positions of power. Fundraising can be fun, and it can be a pain in the butt. Make sure the candidate you are supporting is worth it.

Pros:

- **Support:** Strengthens relationships with legislators.
- **Influence:** Increases your influence with key decision-makers.

Cons:

- **Perception:** Can be perceived as buying influence.
- **Regulation:** Subject to strict fundraising regulations.

> **Pro Tip:** Host creative and engaging events. It's like hosting a themed party—make it memorable and impactful.

16. Social Media Programming

Social media programming can enhance your advocacy efforts by increasing visibility, engagement, and support for your causes. Every legislator is on social media, so it is a great way to get your message out when you have an important vote coming up.

Pros:

- **Reach:** Expands your reach to a broader audience.
- **Engagement:** Facilitates real-time interaction and engagement.

Cons:

- **Management:** Requires ongoing management and content creation.
- **Scrutiny:** Social media activities are highly visible and subject to public scrutiny.

> **Pro Tip:** Stay authentic and interactive. Social media is like a cocktail party—no one likes a wallflower.

17. The Value of AI

I believe in AI. It is your personal lobbying assistant. AI can revolutionize your lobbying efforts by providing powerful tools for data analysis, trend prediction, and operational efficiency just to name a few of AI's capabilities.

Pros:

- **Efficiency:** Automates repetitive tasks, saving time and resources.
- **Insight:** Provides deep insights through data analysis.

Cons:

- **Cost:** Initial setup and implementation can be expensive.
- **Complexity:** Requires understanding and managing advanced technology.

> **Pro Tip:** Embrace AI but always keep a human touch. It's like having a robot vacuum. It's efficient, but you still need to dust the shelves. Use this tool in everything you do. It will save you huge amounts of time planning and strategizing you program

Integrating these seventeen tools into your advocacy toolbox can enhance your lobbying efforts, help you represent your clients more effectively, and help you navigate the legislative landscape with greater confidence and success. Embrace these tools, and you'll be well-equipped to achieve your advocacy goals and make a significant impact in the world of public policy.

Success in lobbying starts with a clear vision—knowing precisely what you want to achieve and mapping out a strategy to make it happen. The next chapter will explore the critical steps in planning, developing strategies, and running effective campaigns. From identifying key objectives to executing targeted actions, understanding how to craft a winning approach is essential. Let's dive into how you as a professional lobbyist turn goals into reality with the right mix of foresight, strategy, and precision.

"Politics is the gentle art of getting votes from the poor and campaign funds from the rich, by promising to protect each from the other."

— Oscar Ameringer

Chapter 19: **Planning, Strategies, and Campaigns**

"Plans are nothing; planning is everything."

— Dwight D. Eisenhower

Welcome to the heart of successful lobbying: planning, strategies, and campaigns. From my experience, I've learned that success in the legislative arena rarely happens by chance. It's the result of careful preparation and deliberate execution. Early in my career, I tried to wing it, thinking a good argument and a bit of persistence would be enough to get the job done. I quickly discovered that without a solid plan to guide my efforts even the best intentions could fall apart. Crafting a comprehensive plan is like building a roadmap. It keeps you focused on the goal, helps you navigate potential obstacles, and ensures you're making the most of your time and resources. Whether it's passing legislation, defeating a harmful bill, or positioning a client for future success, having a clear plan is the foundation for everything else.

Developing strategies and campaigns to achieve a client's goals is where the real art of lobbying comes into play. Each client, issue, and legislative session presents unique challenges, and no two plans are ever the same. I've had to tailor strategies to fit different political climates, personalities, and even unexpected crises that arise mid-session. I once worked on a campaign that hinged on building a coalition of unlikely allies, which required carefully framing the issue to appeal to legislators with vastly different priorities. Another time, success came down to timing—knowing when to push and when to let the process unfold. This chapter is about breaking down these components—planning, strategy, and campaigns—and giving you the tools to master each phase. With the right preparation and execution, you can tackle even the most daunting legislative challenges and come out ahead.

In this chapter you will learn about

- The planning process.
- Developing strategies.
- Case studies.

The Planning Process

Effective lobbying starts with a solid plan. This plan is your roadmap, guiding every action you take to achieve your client's objectives. Here's how to construct it.

Understanding the Legislature

Understanding the legislature involves knowing the legislative calendar, key players, committees, and the procedural rules that govern legislative actions.

Key Points:

- **Legislative Calendar:** Know when sessions are in, critical dates for bill submissions, and vote deadlines.
- **Key Players:** Identify influential legislators, committee chairs, and leaders who can sway decisions.
- **Committees:** Understand which committees will review your issue and their members' interests.
- **Procedural Rules:** Familiarize yourself with the legislative rules to navigate the process effectively.

> **Pro Tip:** Think of the legislature as a complex board game. Knowing the rules and key players allows you to strategize effectively.

Setting Objectives

Clear, achievable objectives are the foundation of any successful lobbying effort. Being S.M.A.R.T. is the way to be.

Key Points:

- **Specific:** Define exactly what you want to accomplish.
- **Measurable:** Ensure you can track progress and measure success.
- **Attainable:** Set realistic goals that are within reach.
- **Relevant:** Align objectives with broader goals and stakeholder interests.
- **Time-Bound:** Set deadlines to create urgency and focus efforts.

Example: Instead of "improving renewable energy policies," set an objective like "pass a bill providing tax incentives for solar energy within the current legislative session."

> *Pro Tip:* Write down your objectives and display them prominently. It's like keeping a treasure map in sight to remind you of the goal.

Research and Analysis

Conduct thorough research on the issue, including historical context, stakeholder identification, and analysis of previous legislative attempts. The more you know the better prepared you will be to pass your legislation.

Key Points:

- **Historical Context:** Understand past efforts and outcomes related to your issue.
- **Stakeholders:** Identify all parties affected by the legislation, including allies and opponents.
- **Data Gathering:** Collect data and facts to support your arguments.
- **Analysis:** Evaluate the data to identify trends, strengths, and weaknesses.

> *Pro Tip:* Think of research as detective work. The more clues you gather, the stronger your case.

Resource Allocation

Identify and allocate resources, including financial, human, and technological tools.

Key Points:

- **Financial Resources:** Budget for lobbying efforts, campaigns, and other expenses.
- **Human Capital:** Identify team members and their roles.
- **Technological Tools:** Utilize data tracking, communication, and campaign management software.

> **Pro Tip:** Allocate resources like a master chef preparing a gourmet meal. Every ingredient (resource) is crucial in the final dish (campaign).

Developing Strategies

With a solid plan, the next step is to develop strategies to guide your actions created by your plan. You can't develop strategy without a detailed plan.

Mapping the Legislative Landscape

Identify key legislators pivotal to your cause, including allies, opposition and those undecided.

Key Points:

- **Supporters:** Identify legislators already in favor of your cause.
- **Opposition:** Know who is against your position and why. Know them inside and out.

- **Undecided:** Target undecided legislators with tailored messages.

> *Pro Tip:* Use a color-coded map to visualize support, opposition, and undecided votes. It's like playing a strategy game where you can see the battlefield.

Building Coalitions

Form alliances with other organizations or groups that share your objectives. Use this tactic only if you need to. Coalitions, while having limited value, can help bring in the numbers to force legislators to know your issue. However, they are hard to manage and sometimes difficult to keep focused.

Key Points:

- **Networking:** Reach out to potential allies and build relationships.
- **Negotiating:** Find common ground and agree on shared goals.
- **Compromising:** Be willing to compromise on minor issues to achieve major goals.

> *Pro Tip:* Building coalitions is like forming a band. Everyone plays a different instrument, but you create a powerful symphony together.

Crafting Your Message

Create a clear, concise, and compelling message highlighting your position's benefits and addressing potential counterarguments.

Key Points:

- **Clarity:** Keep your message simple.
- **Conciseness:** Get to the point quickly.
- **Compelling:** Use data and personal stories to make your case persuasive.

> **Pro Tip:** Craft your message like a great elevator pitch. You should be able to deliver it effectively in the time it takes to ride an elevator It should be one page in length. My rule of thumb is 25 words or less. Brevity is a virtue. .

Engaging Stakeholders

Engage with stakeholders through meetings, briefings, and public forums to keep them informed and involved.

Key Points:

- **Regular Updates:** Keep stakeholders informed of progress and changes.
- **Involvement:** Encourage active participation from stakeholders.
- **Feedback:** Listen to stakeholder feedback and adjust strategies accordingly.

> **Pro Tip:** Engage stakeholders as if hosting a dinner party. Make everyone feel valued and involved. You want to embrace everyone that might be affected by your legislation.

Designing Campaigns

Once your strategies are in place, it's time to design and execute your campaigns.

Legislative Campaigns

A coordinated effort to influence the legislative process through various tactics.

Key Points:

- **Direct Lobbying:** Engage directly with legislators and their staff.
- **Grassroots Mobilization:** Mobilize supporters to advocate for your cause.
- **Media Outreach:** Use media to amplify your message.
- **Public Advocacy:** Educate and engage the public to build support.

> *Pro Tip:* Think of your campaign as a blockbuster movie release. You need trailers (teasers), advertising (media), fan engagement (grassroots), and a strong premiere (legislative action).

Direct Lobbying

Direct interaction with legislators and their staff to present your case.

Key Points:

- **Meetings:** Schedule face-to-face meetings with legislators.
- **Testimony:** Provide testimony at committee hearings.

- **Communication:** Maintain regular contact to keep your issue top of mind.

> **Pro Tip:** Treat direct lobbying like dating. Be charming, genuine, and attentive to build lasting relationships.

Grassroots Mobilization

Mobilize your base to contact legislators, participate in rallies, and engage in advocacy activities.

Key Points:

- **Communication:** Keep your grassroots base informed and motivated.
- **Engagement:** Organize rallies, petitions, and letter-writing campaigns.
- **Support:** Provide resources and guidance to grassroots advocates.

> **Pro Tip:** Think of grassroots mobilization as hosting a flash mob. Surprise, energy, and unity make a powerful statement.

Media Outreach

This is optional. If your client can afford it, take advantage of it. Leverage media to amplify your message through press releases, opinion pieces, interviews, and social media campaigns.

Key Points:

- **Press Releases:** Distribute timely and newsworthy press releases.

- **Opinion Pieces:** Write compelling opinion pieces for publication.

- **Interviews:** Participate in interviews to articulate your message.

- **Social media:** Use social media platforms to reach a broader audience.

> *Pro Tip:* Treat media outreach like baking a cake. Mix the right ingredients (media channels) and give it time to rise (build momentum).

Public Advocacy

Again, this is optional. It depends on the complexity of the issue. Educate and engage the public about your issue through events, campaigns, and online content.

Key Points:

- **Events:** Host public events to raise awareness and gather support.

- **Informational Campaigns:** Run campaigns to educate the public.

- **Online Content:** Create engaging online content to spread your message.

> *Pro Tip:* Approach public advocacy like throwing a festival. Make it informative, engaging, and enjoyable to attract and retain attention.

Monitoring and Adaptation

The legislative landscape shift rapidly, so constant monitoring and the ability to adapt are crucial.

Tracking Progress

Constantly monitor your campaign's progress and adapt as needed.

Key Points:

- **Bill Tracking:** Keep track of the bill's progress through the legislature.
- **Feedback:** Gather feedback from stakeholders and adapt strategies.
- **Flexibility:** Be prepared to adjust your plan based on new developments.

> **Pro Tip:** Think of monitoring and adaptation as steering a ship. Constantly check your course and adjust the sails to navigate smoothly.

Case Study: Successful Campaign

Let's look at a hypothetical case study to illustrate these principles in action.

Objective: Pass a bill that provides tax incentives for renewable energy projects.

Planning:

- **Understand the Legislature:** Know the legislative calendar, key committees, and influential legislators.

- **Set Objectives:** Pass the bill within the current legislative session.
- **Research and Analysis:** Gather data on the benefits of renewable energy, previous legislative attempts, and current opposition arguments.
- **Resource Allocation:** Allocate the budget for lobbying efforts, media campaigns, and grassroots mobilization.

Strategy:

- **Map the Landscape:** Identify key supporters and potential swing votes.
- **Build Coalitions:** Partner with environmental groups, business associations, and community organizations.
- **Craft the Message:** Highlight economic benefits, job creation, and environmental impact.
- **Engage Stakeholders:** Hold briefings with key stakeholders and legislators.

Campaign:

- **Direct Lobbying:** Schedule meetings with legislators, provide testimony at hearings, and maintain ongoing communication.
- **Grassroots Mobilization:** Mobilize supporters to contact legislators and participate in rallies.
- **Media Outreach:** Issue press releases, write opinion pieces, and engage with media outlets.
- **Public Advocacy:** Host public events, run social media campaigns, and distribute informational materials.

Monitoring and Adaptation:

- **Track Bill Progress:** Constantly monitor the bill's progress and adapt strategies.

- **Respond to Opposition:** Address opposition arguments with updated data and testimonials.

- **Maintain Flexibility:** Be ready to adapt to any legislative changes or new developments.

Effective lobbying requires meticulous planning, strategic thinking, and coordinated campaigns. Understanding the legislative process, setting clear objectives, developing robust strategies, and designing impactful campaigns can significantly enhance your chances of achieving your client's desired outcomes. Embrace these principles, and you'll be well equipped to navigate the complex world of legislative advocacy with confidence and success.

Remember, a well-executed plan is your strongest tool in lobbying. Like a seasoned chef, you must skillfully combine ingredients (strategies) to create a masterpiece (successful campaign).

Effective lobbying hinges on strong communication with legislators, regulators, and their staff, who hold the power to shape policy. The next chapter will explore how to engage these key players, convey your message clearly, and build the relationships needed to move your agenda forward. Understanding how to communicate with each group is crucial for navigating the political process and ensuring your voice is heard where it matters most. Let's dive into the strategies for making those connections count.

"Politics is too important to be left to the politicians."

— Charles de Gaulle

Chapter 20: **Are You Receiving, Houston?**

"It's not what you say, it's what people hear. If you want to impact public opinion, you must communicate your message clearly and effectively, in a way that resonates with people's values and emotions."

— *Frank Luntz*

Communicating your message to legislators, regulators, and their staff can sometimes feel like transmitting signals into the vast unknown, hoping for a response. Early in my career, I naively assumed that just having a strong argument or a well-written position paper was enough to get results. I quickly realized that even the most compelling message will fall flat if it's not delivered in the right way to the right people at the right time. Each audience—whether it's a legislator, a regulatory official, or their staff—has unique priorities, pressures, and perspectives that shape how they receive information. I've had meetings where a straightforward data-driven pitch worked perfectly, and others where it took a story about real-world impacts to get my point across. The challenge is learning how to adjust your message to fit the recipient while staying true to your core objectives.

Delivering a message is as much about connection as it is about content. I've learned that the way you frame your message is just as important as what you're saying. Legislators, for example, are juggling hundreds of competing demands, so I make it a point to be clear, concise, and show them how the issue directly impacts their constituents. With staff, who often act as gatekeepers, I focus on building rapport and ensuring they have everything they need to brief their boss effectively. Regulators, on the other hand, often value technical expertise and solutions-oriented approaches. It's a delicate balance, but once you master the art of tailoring your communication to your audience, your signals no longer get lost in the void. Instead, they resonate—and that's how you build support and make meaningful progress. In this chapter, we'll break down how to craft, refine, and deliver your message so it lands exactly where it needs to. Buckle up! Legislative communication is about to become a whole lot clearer.

In this chapter you will learn about

- Knowing your audience.
- Crafting your message to your audience.
- Delivering your message to your audience.
- Making your message stick.
- Understanding communication breakdowns.
- Using humor to lighten the message.

Know Your Audience: The Decision-Makers

Before crafting your message, you must understand who you're communicating with. Legislators, regulators, and their staff are not monoliths. Each has its own priorities, pet issues, and communication styles. Tailoring your message to fit the audience is the first step in ensuring it's received and understood.

Legislators: The Elected Officials

Various factors, including party affiliation, constituent needs, and personal beliefs drive legislators. They are often pressed for time and must manage multiple issues simultaneously.

Key Points:

- **Style:** Be concise and direct. Legislators appreciate brevity combined with clarity.
- **Medium:** In-person meetings, phone calls, and brief, well-organized memos.
- **Delivery:** Tie your issue to their district's interests. Highlight voter impact and potential media attention and align with their known stances.
- **Education Level:** How far did they go in their education. Important item.

Pro Tip: Think of communicating with legislators like speed dating. You have limited time to make a strong, memorable impression.

Regulators: The Rule-Makers

Regulators implement and enforce the public policy created by the legislature. They tend to focus more on the technical details and implications of policies. There can be a disconnect between the legislator's intended purpose of the legislation passed and the interpretation made by the regulator. This makes communication critical to ensure the desired intent.

Key Points:

- **Style:** Detailed and technical but still accessible. Focus on data and evidence.
- **Medium:** Detailed reports, technical papers, and formal presentations.
- **Delivery:** Emphasize how your issue aligns with regulatory goals and the broader public interest.

> **Pro Tip:** Engaging with regulators is like preparing a science fair project. Your presentation should be thorough, well researched, and clear.

Legislative Staff: The Gatekeepers

Staff members are crucial in the decision-making process. They filter and interpret information for their bosses. Everything you send to your legislator goes through a staffer.

Key Points:

- **Style:** Clear and well structured. Staff appreciate having all the relevant details.
- **Medium:** Emails, briefings, and fact sheets.
- **Delivery:** Establish a relationship. Be respectful of their role and time constraints. Please provide them with all the tools they need to champion your issue.

> **Pro Tip:** Treat legislative staff like VIP concierges. They can make or break your access to decision-makers.

Crafting the Message: Substance and Style

The substance of your message is crucial but so is the style in which it's delivered. The best messages are memorable, persuasive, and easy to understand.

Substance: What to Say

Key Points:

- **Clear Objective:** Start with clearly stating what you want. Make your ask explicit.
- **Supporting Facts:** Use data, anecdotes, and expert opinions to support your point.
- **Relevance:** Explain why the issue matters to the decision-maker and their constituents.

> **Pro Tip:** Think of your message as a sandwich. Start with what you want (the top bun), add the meat (supporting facts), and finish with why it matters (the bottom bun).

Style: How to Say It

Key Points:

- **Simplicity:** Avoid jargon. Use plain language to ensure your message is accessible.
- **Brevity:** Keep it short. Decision-makers don't have time to wade through long documents.

- **Persuasion:** Use rhetorical techniques like storytelling, analogies, and metaphors to make your message stick.

> **Pro Tip:** Deliver your message like a tweet—clear, concise, and compelling in 280 characters or less. Brevity is a virtue. Legislators appreciate short, concise messages.

The Medium: Channeling Your Message

Choosing the right medium is as important as the message itself. Different situations call for different approaches.

In-Person Meetings

Face-to-face communication is often the most effective. It allows for immediate feedback and the opportunity to build a personal connection. Always go to for an in-person meeting. It is by far the most effective way to handle your issue and get results.

Key Points:

- **Preparation:** Know your facts and anticipate questions.
- **Presentation:** Be engaging. Use visuals if possible.
- **Follow-up:** Always follow up with a thank-you note and any additional information requested.

> **Pro Tip:** Treat in-person meetings like job interviews. Dress well, be punctual, and make a great first impression. Your job is to clarify public policy and achieve a mutual understanding of what was passed and how it will be correctly implemented.

Written Communication

When done right, written communication leaves a lasting impression.

Key Points:

- **Emails:** Clear subject lines, concise content, and a call to action.
- **Memos:** Structured with headings, bullet points, and a summary.
- **Reports:** Detailed, with an executive summary for quick reading.

> **Pro Tip:** Writing is like cooking—use simple, high-quality ingredients (clear language) for the best results.

Digital Channels

Social media, webinars, and online forums are increasingly crucial in our digital age.

Key Points:

- **Social media:** Use for quick updates and to show public support.
- **Webinars:** Great for detailed presentations to a broad audience.
- **Online Forums:** Engage with decision-makers in public discussions to raise awareness.

> **Pro Tip:** Think of digital channels as your megaphone. Use them to amplify your message far and wide.

Delivery: Making It Stick

The delivery of your message can make or break its effectiveness. Here's how to ensure your message is received loud and clear.

Timing

Timing is everything. Understanding the legislative calendar and the decision-maker's schedule is crucial.

Key Points:

- **Legislative Sessions:** Know when sessions are in progress and when decisions are likely to be made.
- **Deadlines:** Be aware of submission deadlines for reports, proposals, and other documents.

> *Pro Tip:* Timing your communication is like hitting a baseball. You must swing right to knock it out of the park.

Personalization

Personalize your communication to make it more impactful.

Key Points:

- **Personal Address:** Always use the decision-maker's name.
- **Reference Past Interactions:** If you've met before, reference previous conversations to build rapport.
- **Tailor to Interests:** Mention issues you know the decision-maker cares about.

> **Pro Tip:** Personalization is like writing a love let-
> ter. Make it specific, heartfelt, and relevant to the
> recipient.

Follow-Up

Always remember the power of a follow-up.

Key Points:

- **Thank-You Notes:** A simple thank-you can go a long way in building goodwill.
- **Additional Information:** If new data or reports come out, share them.
- **Continued Engagement:** Keep the lines of communication open. Regular updates can keep your issue top of mind.

> **Pro Tip:** Follow-ups are like watering a plant. Consis-
> tent care helps your relationship grow. A thank-you
> note solidifies your relationship with the legislator or
> the regulator. It shows your appreciation for the time
> spent working on the issue and the cooperation you
> shared. Such a simple act of professionalism goes a
> long way.

Communication Breakdowns: Why It Happen and How to Avoid Them

Despite your best efforts, communication can sometimes be misunderstood. Here's why and how to prevent it.

The Translation Problem

When transmitting your message, it can get lost in translation due to differences in language, interpretation, and background.

Key Points:

- **Jargon:** Avoid technical language that may not be understood.
- **Assumptions:** Don't assume the decision-maker has the same knowledge base as you.
- **Clarity:** Be clear about what you're asking and why it's important.

> *Pro Tip:* Think of communication like playing the game Telephone. Ensure clarity to avoid the message being misinterpreted as it is passed along.

Feedback Loop

Create a feedback loop to ensure your message is understood.

Key Points:

- **Ask for Feedback:** After delivering your message, ask if any questions or clarifications are needed.
- **Summarize:** At the end of a meeting, summarize the key points and the next steps.
- **Follow-up:** Send a follow-up email summarizing the discussion and action items.

> **Pro Tip:** A feedback loop is like checking your rear-view mirror while driving. It helps ensure you're on the right track.

Listening

Effective communication is a two-way street. Listening is as critical as talking.

Key Points:

- **Active Listening:** Show you're listening by nodding, making eye contact, and summarizing points.
- **Empathy:** Understand the decision-maker's perspective and concerns.
- **Adaptability:** Be ready to adjust your message based on the feedback received.

> **Pro Tip:** Listening is like dancing. Pay attention to your partner's moves to keep in sync.

Humor: The Secret Ingredient

A little humor can make your message memorable, but it must be used wisely.

Key Points:

- **Know Your Audience:** Ensure your humor is appropriate for the audience.
- **Lighten the Mood:** Use humor to break the ice and make the conversation more enjoyable.

- **Be Relatable:** Self-deprecating humor can make you more relatable, but don't overdo it.

> **Pro Tip:** Think of humor like seasoning. Just the right amount enhances the flavor, but more is needed to ensure the dish is good.

Houston, We Have Contact

Communicating with legislators, regulators, and their staff requires a blend of strategy, clarity, and adaptability. By understanding your audience, crafting a clear and persuasive message, choosing the right medium, and delivering it effectively, you can ensure your message is received loud and clear. Avoiding communication breakdowns and adding a touch of humor can further enhance your efforts.

Do you know your opposition? Do you know what they think? What is their plan for defeating your legislation? These are just some items we will cover in the next chapter. You must know your opposition better than yourself to defeat their campaign against you and the issues you represent.

"The most important political office is that of the private citizen."

— Louis D. Brandeis

Chapter 21: Don't Shoot till You See the Whites of Their Eyes

"One of the cardinal rules in lobbying is to know your opposition better than you know yourself. Understanding their arguments, strategies, and weaknesses is essential to shaping a winning message and outmaneuvering them in the legislative process."

— *Gerald S.J. Cassidy*

I n the gladiatorial arena of lobbying, understanding your opposition is absolutely essential—it's not just about knowing who disagrees with you but why. Early in my career, I made the mistake of underestimating an opposing group, thinking their argument lacked merit and their support was weak. I soon found out the hard way that they had cultivated relationships and built alliances behind the scenes, putting my client's interests in jeopardy. That experience taught me a valuable lesson: knowing your adversaries is half the battle. Whether it's a competing association, a legislator with an opposing viewpoint, or a regulatory body hesitant to act, the key is to understand their motivations, strengths, and weaknesses. Are they driven by ideology, personal relationships, or constituent pressure? Once you know what makes them tick, you can strategize accordingly and anticipate their moves.

Gathering intel on your opposition is like going on a reconnaissance mission—you have to be thorough, strategic, and sometimes creative. I've spent hours digging into public testimony, analyzing voting records, and learning about the alliances that shape an opponent's influence. I've sat in committee hearings just to observe how opposing groups frame their arguments or tailor their messaging. This kind of preparation allows you to neutralize their strengths and exploit their weaknesses, whether it's countering misinformation, building a stronger coalition, or crafting a more compelling narrative. In one particularly contentious campaign, understanding the opposition's motivations helped me reframe our argument to appeal to undecided legislators, ultimately securing the votes we needed. This chapter is about mastering that art of reconnaissance—because when you know your adversaries inside and out, you're no longer playing defense. You're positioning yourself to win. Let's dive in and get ready for the battle ahead!

In this chapter you will about

- Knowing your enemy.
- Mapping relationships.
- Leveraging Information.
- Strategy for legislative campaigns.

Know Thy Enemy: The Importance of Intel

In *The Art of War*, Sun Tzu famously said, "If you know the enemy and know yourself, you need not fear the result of a hundred battles." The same holds in the legislative arena. Understanding your opposition's motivations, tactics, and alliances can provide a decisive advantage.

Identifying the Opposition

The first step is to identify who opposes your issue. This could be:

- Competing interest groups or associations
- Individual legislators or regulators with conflicting agendas
- Business rivals
- Community organizations or advocacy groups

Once identified, categorize your opposition based on their influence and resources. Not all opponents are created equal; some may be vocal but lack real power, while others might wield significant influence quietly.

> **Pro Tip:** Think of categorizing your opposition like sorting laundry—separate the whites (most influential) from the colors (less influential) to determine where to apply the most effort.

Research: Digging Deep

Effective research is the cornerstone of understanding your opposition. Here's how to dive deep into the background and current activities of those who stand against you.

Public Records and Documents

Start with the basics: public records and documents can reveal a lot of information.

- **Legislative Records:** Review voting records, bill sponsorships, and public statements of opposing legislators.
- **Regulatory Filings:** Examine filings with regulatory agencies to understand the stance of opposing regulators or businesses.
- **Financial Disclosures:** To follow the money trail, look at campaign finance reports, lobbying disclosures, and corporate financial statements.

Pro Tip: Think of this as detective work. Every piece of information is a clue that helps you understand your opposition better.

News and Media

Stay informed through news outlets, press releases, and media coverage.

- **News Articles:** Track recent news articles mentioning your opposition. This helps gauge public sentiment and recent activities.
- **Press Releases:** Review press releases from opposition groups to understand their messaging and upcoming actions.
- **Social media:** Monitor channels for real-time updates and insights into their strategies and support base.

Pro Tip: Use social media monitoring tools to streamline this process. It's like having a radar that pings whenever your opposition makes a move. Schedule AI to scan the press to find the information on your opposition,

Industry Reports and White Papers

Industry reports and white papers can offer in-depth analyses and predictions.

- **Industry Publications:** Subscribe to industry-specific publications that might feature your opposition.
- **Think Tanks and Research Institutes:** Leverage reports from think tanks and research institutes that analyze legislative and regulatory trends.

> *Pro Tip:* Think of these reports as treasure maps. They can provide valuable insights into your opposition's strategies and weaknesses. Use AI to scan the report and white papers to give you the key points.

Mapping Relationships: The Legislative Web

Understanding your opposition's network is crucial. Relationships often dictate influence and decision-making in the legislative and regulatory arenas.

Lobbyist Connections

Identify the lobbyists representing your opposition. Lobbyists often have deep connections and can be pivotal players.

- **Lobbying Registrations:** Check lobbying registration databases to see who is registered to lobby on behalf of your opposition.
- **Client Lists:** Review lobbyist client lists to identify potential alliances and conflicts of interest.

> *Pro Tip:* To see the full picture, consider using AI tools that map out these connections visually, like a spider web.

Legislative Relationships

Map out relationships between legislators and your opposition.

- **Committee Memberships:** Legislators on key committees often hold significant sway. Determine which committees your opposition influences.

- **Caucus Memberships:** Identify any caucuses or informal groups that your opposition might belong to. These affiliations can reveal their legislative allies.

> **Pro Tip:** Track these relationships using a color-coded chart. It's like creating a playbook to understand who's who in the legislative arena.

Regulatory Ties

Understand the connections between your opposition and regulatory bodies.

- **Advisory Panels:** Check if your opposition is part of any advisory panels or working groups within regulatory agencies.

- **Public Comments:** Review public comments submitted by your opposition on regulatory proposals to understand their stance and influence.

> **Pro Tip:** Think of this as creating a detailed map before a treasure hunt. The more you know about the terrain (relationships), the better you can navigate it.

Leveraging Information: Turning Intel into Advantage

Armed with comprehensive information about your opposition, the next step is to use it to your advantage. Here's how to strategize and execute your legislative campaign.

Crafting the Message

Tailor your message to highlight the weaknesses of your opposition and the strengths of your position.

- **Contrasting Narratives:** Create a narrative that contrasts your solution's benefits with the pitfalls of the opposition's stance.
- **Data-Driven Arguments:** Use data to undermine the opposition's claims. Facts and figures can be powerful tools to sway undecided stakeholders.

> **Pro Tip:** Think of your message like a superhero origin story. It should be compelling and relatable and highlight your strengths, which set you apart from the opposition.

Building Coalitions

Leverage your network to build coalitions that can amplify your message.

- **Allied Groups:** Identify and collaborate with groups that share your interests. There is strength in numbers; more allies can make a significant impact.
- **Bipartisan Support:** Aim to secure support from both sides of the aisle. A bipartisan approach can neutralize partisan opposition.

> **Pro Tip:** Building coalitions is like organizing a pot-luck dinner. Everyone brings something to the table, and together you create a feast.

Engaging the Media

Use the media to shape public perception and put pressure on decision-makers.

- **Op-Eds and Editorials:** Write op-eds and editorials to highlight the benefits of your position and the drawbacks of the opposition's stance.
- **Press Conferences:** Hold press conferences to announce new endorsements or present compelling evidence that supports your cause.

> **Pro Tip:** Treat media engagement like a performance. Practice your lines, know your cues, and always be ready for the spotlight.

Strategies for the Legislative Campaign

Deploying effective strategies is crucial to outmaneuver your opposition. Here are some tactics to consider.

Grassroots Mobilization

Engage the public to build grassroots support that can influence legislators and regulators.

- **Petitions and Letter-Writing Campaigns:** Organize petitions and letter-writing campaigns to demonstrate widespread support.

- **Town Halls and Public Forums:** Host town halls and forums to educate the public and galvanize support.

> **Pro Tip:** Think of grassroots mobilization as starting a fire. Begin with kindling (small actions) and build up to a roaring blaze (widespread support).

Direct Lobbying

- Direct lobbying efforts can be highly effective when well-executed.
- **One-on-One Meetings:** Arrange meetings with key legislators and regulators to present your case personally.
- **Legislative Hearings:** Testify at legislative hearings to provide expert opinions and counter the opposition's arguments.

> **Pro Tip:** Approach direct lobbying like preparing for a debate. Know your points, anticipate counterarguments, and be ready to defend your position passionately.

Intelligence Countermeasures

Anticipate and neutralize the opposition's moves with intelligence countermeasures.

- **Monitoring:** Continuously monitor the opposition's activities and be ready to respond quickly.
- **Discrediting:** If appropriate, discredit the opposition by highlighting conflicts of interest, past failures, or misinformation.

- **Documents:** Collect copies of literature that is distributed to legislators expressing their viewpoint. This will tell you what their message is the strategies they are using.

> ⚒ **Pro Tip:** Think of intelligence countermeasures as playing chess. Always be a few moves ahead of your opponent.

Case Study: A Tactical Win

To illustrate these concepts, let's consider a hypothetical case study in which a lobbyist successfully used these strategies to outmaneuver the opposition.

The Issue

A lobbyist advocates for renewable energy incentives, facing opposition from a powerful fossil fuel lobby.

Research and Intel

The lobbyist starts by:

- **Identifying Key Opponents:** Major fossil fuel companies and their lobbying firms.
- **Analyzing Voting Records:** Reviewing legislators' voting records to identify potential swing votes.
- **Mapping Relationships:** Uncovering connections between fossil fuel lobbyists and key legislators.

Strategy Development

With intel in hand, the lobbyist crafts a strategy:

- **Tailored Messaging:** This messaging emphasizes job creation and the economic benefits of renewable energy, countering the opposition's economic arguments.
- **Coalition Building:** Forms a coalition with environmental groups, labor unions, and businesses in the renewable sector.
- **Media Engagement:** Publishes op-eds highlighting renewable energy's public health benefits and the negative impact of the fossil fuel industry.

Execution

The lobbyist:

- **Mobilizes Grassroots Support:** Launches a petition campaign and organizes public rallies.
- **Directly Lobbies Legislators:** Holds one-on-one meetings with undecided legislators, presenting compelling data and constituent support.
- **Counters Opposition:** Monitors opposition moves and quickly discredits false claims with factual rebuttals.

Outcome

Combining thorough research, strategic coalition-building, compelling messaging, and media engagement leads to a legislative victory for renewable energy incentives. The fossil fuel lobby is outmaneuvered, and the bill passes with bipartisan support.

Ready, Aim, Advocate

Understanding and outmaneuvering your opposition in the legislative arena requires a blend of strategic intelligence, tailored communication, and effective execution. By knowing your opposition better than they know themselves, you can anticipate their moves, counter their arguments, and rally support for your cause.

As you prepare for your next legislative campaign, remember Sun Tzu's words: "In the midst of chaos, there is also opportunity." Use your knowledge of the opposition to turn challenges into opportunities, and you'll be well on your way to legislative victory. And remember, a touch of humor can go a long way in easing tensions and building rapport.

In today's fast-paced world, managing the media is just as crucial as managing relationships with legislators. The right message, delivered through the right platform, can shape public opinion and influence policy decisions. In chapter 22, we'll explore the intricacies of working with media platforms, from building relationships with reporters to navigating social media. Get ready to learn how to craft your message and use the media to your advantage in the ever-evolving public relations landscape.

"Patriotism is supporting your country all the time,
and your government when it deserves it."

— Mark Twain

Chapter 22: Managing Media Platforms

"In today's legislative campaigns, you have to know how to leverage media platforms effectively. Whether it's traditional media or social media, controlling the narrative and getting your message out through the right channels can make or break your effort to influence legislation."

— *Tony Podesta*

E ffectively communicating your message to legislators and regulators has always been a critical part of lobbying, but the tools and platforms we use have evolved dramatically over the years. I've come through the era of no cell phones and no computers, where communication was slower, more deliberate, and heavily reliant on face-to-face meetings, handwritten notes, and the occasional phone call from a landline. Back then, the media landscape was simpler. The local newspaper, radio, or evening news were your main avenues to reach a broader audience. Today, the media landscape is a completely different beast, with social media, twenty-four-hour news cycles, and digital platforms shaping public opinion in real time. I've learned to adapt, using these modern tools to amplify my message, but the fundamentals remain the same: a clear, compelling story is still at the heart of effective communication, no matter what era or platform you're working in.

Navigating today's media ecosystem requires both strategy and agility, and I've had to learn how to use these new tools to stay relevant and effective. Building relationships with reporters remains just as important as it was decades ago. They need reliable sources who can provide clear, accurate information, and that trust can result in positive coverage for your issue. At the same time, social media offers an incredible opportunity to bypass traditional gatekeepers and speak directly to the public. I've run campaigns that combined media interviews, press releases, and viral social media posts to build momentum for my clients' causes. While the platforms have changed, the message must always be consistent, concise, and impactful. Whether I'm leveraging a tweet, pitching a story to a journalist, or working with a public relations firm to shape a broader campaign, the goal is always the same: to ensure the issue gets the attention it deserves and drives meaningful action. In this chapter, we'll explore how to master this balance of old-school relationship-building and modern media strategies to communicate effectively in today's fast-paced world.

In this chapter you will learn about

- The different media platforms.
- Building relationships with reporters.
- PR campaigns.
- Managing the message.

Definition of Media Platforms

Media platforms are the channels through which information is disseminated to the public. They include traditional outlets such as newspapers, television, radio, and digital platforms like news websites, blogs, and social media. Each platform has its audience, style, and method of communication. Understanding these nuances is essential for tailoring your message effectively.

> **Pro Tip:** Think of media platforms as different tools in your lobbying toolbox. Each tool has its specific use and knowing which one to use can make all the difference in getting the job done right.

The Difference Between Social Media and the Press

While social media and traditional press serve as conduits for information, they operate differently.

Traditional Press

Traditional press, which includes newspapers, magazines, television, and radio is often seen as more credible and authoritative. It relies on established journalistic practices and editorial oversight.

Pros:

- **Credibility:** Due to rigorous fact-checking and editorial standards.
- **Depth:** Allows for in-depth reporting and analysis.
- **Audience Trust:** Readers often view these sources as reliable.

Cons:

- **Speed:** Slower to publish compared to social media.

- **Accessibility:** Can be less accessible to the public for immediate updates.

Social Media

Social media platforms like X, Facebook, LinkedIn, and Instagram allow for direct engagement with your audience and real-time updates. However, the lack of editorial control can lead to the spread of misinformation.

Pros:

- **Immediacy:** Real-time updates and instant communication.

- **Engagement:** Direct interaction with your audience.

- **Reach:** Potential for widespread and viral dissemination.

Cons:

- **Credibility Issues:** Higher potential for misinformation.

- **Control:** Less control over how the message is interpreted and shared.

> *Pro Tip:* Use traditional press for credibility and depth and social media for speed and engagement. It's like using a flashlight (press) for a focused beam of light and a lantern (social media) for broad illumination.

Building Relationships with Reporters

Reporters are gatekeepers to the press, and building solid relationships with them is vital. Start by identifying the journalists who cover your industry or issue. Follow their work, understand their interests, and engage with them respectfully.

Steps to Building Strong Relationships

- **Research Reporters:** Identify who covers your industry and issues.
- **Engage Respectfully:** Follow their work and engage meaningfully.
- **Offer Value:** Be a reliable and credible source of information.
- **Maintain Availability:** Be responsive and transparent.
- **Build Trust:** Over time, prove your reliability and credibility.

> **Pro Tip:** Treat building relationships with reporters like cultivating a garden. It takes time, attention, and care, but the fruits of your labor will be rewarding.

How to Get Coverage of Your Issue

Securing media coverage requires a strategic approach. Here are some steps to follow:

Craft a Compelling Story

Reporters are looking for stories that resonate with their audience. Frame your issue to highlight its importance and relevance.

Press Releases

Write clear, concise press releases that provide all necessary information. Include quotes from key stakeholders and data to support your claims.

Tips for Effective Press Releases

- **Headline:** Make it catchy and informative.
- **Lead:** Provide the most crucial information upfront.
- **Body:** Include supporting details, quotes, and data.
- **Contact Info:** Ensure reporters can reach you for more information.

Media Kits

Prepare comprehensive media kits with background information, high-quality images, and contact details.

> **Pro Tip:** Think of media kits like a goodie bag at a party. Give reporters everything they need to cover your story.

Pitching

Tailor your pitches to individual reporters. Explain why your story is relevant to their audience and provide exclusive insights or interviews.

Follow-Up

Don't hesitate to follow up if you don't receive a response. However, be respectful of the reporter's time and deadlines.

> **Pro Tip:** Think of following up like gentle persistence in sales. It's okay to be persistent but don't become a pest.

What Reporters Want from You to Get Them to Cover Your Issue

Reporters are inundated with story ideas every day. To cut through the noise, you need to provide them with:

Newsworthy Content: Ensure your story is timely, relevant, and impactful.

Clarity: Present your information clearly and concisely. Avoid jargon and provide context.

Credibility: Offer credible sources, data, and evidence to back up your claims.

Accessibility: Be available for follow-up questions and provide additional resources if needed.

Exclusivity: Offering an exclusive story or angle can make your pitch more attractive.

> *Pro Tip:* Think of what reporters want like a recipe. Follow the steps correctly, and you'll have a dish (story) that everyone wants to taste (cover).

PR Campaigns

Public relations (PR) campaigns are coordinated efforts to communicate a specific message to a target audience. These campaigns can include press releases, media outreach, events, engagement, and more. The goal is to create a cohesive narrative that advances your objectives. As the lobbyist you can direct the PR campaign because you know the audience and what they need to hear to get them to consider the issue. Also, not all issues need a campaign. The issue, its importance, and economic impact dictates the creation of a PR program.

Planning a PR Campaign

Objectives: Define clear goals for what you want to achieve.

Target Audience: Identify who you need to reach and tailor your message accordingly.

Strategy: Develop a plan that includes key messages, tactics, and a timeline.

Execution: Implement your plan precisely, monitoring progress and adjusting as needed.

Evaluation: Measure the success of your campaign and analyze what worked and what didn't.

> *Pro Tip:* Think of a PR campaign like planning a road trip. You need a destination (objective), a map (strategy), and checkpoints (evaluation) to ensure you stay on course.

Using a Public Relations Firm and the Cost Associated with the Campaign

Hiring a public relations firm can provide expertise and resources that enhance your campaign's effectiveness. PR firms offer media relations, crisis management, content creation, and strategic planning services.

Costs of Hiring a PR Firm

Costs can vary widely depending on the scope of the campaign and the firm's reputation. Here are some common pricing structures:

Retainers: A monthly fee for ongoing services, typically ranging from $2,000 to $20,000 or more.

Project-Based Fees: A one-time fee for a specific project can range from $5,000 to $50,000 or more.

Hourly Rates: Fees are based on the time spent on your campaign, typically ranging from $100 to $500 per hour.

> **Pro Tip:** Hiring a PR firm is like hiring a wedding planner. They bring expertise and can handle the details, but it comes at a cost.

Social Media vs. the Press

The choice between social media and traditional press depends on your objectives and audience. Here's a comparison:

Reach

- **Social media:** Immediate, widespread reach and the ability to engage directly with your audience.
- **Press:** Provides credibility and depth.

Speed

- **Social media:** Allows for real-time updates.
- **Press:** Follows a more deliberate publishing schedule.

Control

- **Social media:** More control over your message but more prone to public scrutiny and backlash.
- **Press:** Involves third-party validation but less control over the final narrative.

Engagement

- **Social media:** Fosters direct interaction.

- **Press:** Relies on one-way communication.

> *Pro Tip:* Use a balanced approach that leverages the strengths of both platforms for the best results.

Managing the Message to Have the Most Dynamic Effect

To maximize the impact of your message, consider the following strategies:

Consistency: Ensure your message is consistent across all platforms and communications.

Clarity: Keep your message clear and focused. Avoid unnecessary complexity.

Storytelling: Use storytelling to make your message more relatable and memorable.

Visuals: Incorporate visuals such as images, videos, and infographics to enhance engagement.

Adaptability: Be ready to adapt your message in response to feedback and changing circumstances.

Measurement: Track the performance of your message using AI analytics and adjust your strategy as needed.

> *Pro Tip:* Managing your message is like conducting an orchestra. Ensure all the instruments (platforms) play harmoniously to create a beautiful symphony (effective communication).

Effectively working with media platforms is a critical skill for any lobbyist. By understanding the differences between social media and the press, building solid relationships with reporters, securing coverage, and managing your message strategically, you can ensure your issue garners the attention it deserves. Whether you're running a PR campaign or navigating the intricacies of social media, the insights provided in this chapter will equip you with the tools you need to succeed in the dynamic world of media relations.

Remember, mastering media platforms is like learning to ride a bike. It might be tricky at first, but once you get the hang of it, you'll navigate the landscape with confidence and ease.

Technology—you can love it or hate it—is effective when running your legislative campaign. As a lobbyist, you must master it to win. In the next two chapters, we will delve into technology, explain it, and show you how to use it effectively.

"Liberty means responsibility. That is why most men dread it."

— George Bernard Shaw

Chapter 23: Identifying Technology Sources

"In today's legislative landscape, the successful lobbyist strategically harnesses the power of technology
to gather actionable insights, mobilize grassroots
support, and drive strategic advocacy. By leveraging
advanced tools and data-driven strategies, we can
influence policy and create more informed and engaged communities, giving us a competitive edge in
the legislative process."

—John Ashford,
Founder and CEO of the Hawthorn Group

In the ever-changing world of lobbying, staying ahead of the curve
is not just important—it's critical. I've seen industry evolve from
an era where everything was done by hand or in person, to one
where technology drives almost every aspect of the work. When I
first started, gathering information meant physically digging through
files, visiting offices, and relying on word of mouth to track legislation. Today, with bill-tracking software, legislative databases, and

instant communication tools, I can monitor a bill's progress, research lawmakers' voting records, and identify key stakeholders all from my phone or computer. Technology has not only streamlined how I gather information but also enhanced how I mobilize support. I've used email campaigns, virtual meetings, and even social media to rally advocates and connect them directly with lawmakers in ways that were impossible in the past.

But with all the advantages technology brings, I've also learned that it's a tool, not a replacement for the fundamentals of lobbying. Technology can help you disseminate your message quickly and efficiently, but it's still up to you to ensure the message resonates. For instance, while social media can raise awareness and rally grassroots support, a personal meeting with a legislator or a well-crafted briefing often carries more weight in influencing decision-making. I've seen firsthand how over-relying on technology without strategic thinking can backfire, leading to fragmented efforts and missed opportunities. The key is knowing when and how to use these tools to complement your overall strategy. In the next two chapters, we'll explore the specific technologies available to lobbyists, their pros and cons, and how to use them effectively to gather information, mobilize allies, and achieve meaningful legislative results.

In this chapter your will learn about

- Information technology.
- Technology for mobilizing proponents.
- Technology for achieving desired outcomes.
- Using technology to motivate proponents.
- Case studies: successful technology-driven lobbying campaigns.
- Ethical considerations and best practices.

Technology for Information Gathering

Advanced Research Tools: Legis info Platforms (e.g., GovTrack, LegiScan):

Advantages:

- Provides comprehensive access to legislative data, including bill texts, status, and voting records.
- Offers real-time updates and alerts on legislative activities.

Disadvantages:

- Subscription costs for premium features.
- Can be overwhelming due to the volume of information.

AI-Powered Research Assistants (e.g., Chat GPT, Copilot):

Advantages:

- Quickly analyzes and summarizes large volumes of legislative documents.
- Identifies relevant connections and insights within the data.

Disadvantages:

- Requires training to fine-tune accuracy.
- May miss nuances in complex legislative language.
- Must verify its contents.

Social Media Monitoring Tools (e.g., Hootsuite, Brand Watch):

Advantages:

- Tracks real-time public sentiment and discussions around legislative issues.
- Identifies vital influencers and trending topics.
- Provides data on engagement metrics and audience demographics.
- Integrates data from multiple sources into a single platform.
- Provides powerful visualization tools to identify trends and patterns.
- Facilitates informed decision-making with comprehensive dashboards.

Disadvantages:

- Privacy concerns regarding data collection.
- High cost for advanced features and comprehensive coverage.
- Steep learning curve for new users.
- Requires significant data management and integration efforts.

Technology for Mobilizing Proponents

Automated Email Campaign Tools (e.g., Mailchimp, Constant Contact):

Advantages:

- Allows for segmented and targeted messaging.

- Automates follow-ups and reminders.
- Provides analytics on open rates, click-through rates, and engagement.

Disadvantages:

- The risk of being marked as spam if not properly managed.
- Requires careful crafting to avoid generic or impersonal messaging.

Social Media Advocacy Platforms (e.g., Nation Builder, Muster):

Advantages:

- Engages supporters through social media channels.
- Provides tools for grassroots mobilization and petition drives.
- Tracks supporter engagement and campaign progress.

Disadvantages:

- Can be time-consuming to manage multiple platforms.
- Public backlash if not handled with authenticity and transparency.

Text Messaging Campaign Tools (e.g., Hustle, EZ Texting):

Advantages:

- High open and response rates compared to email.
- Allows for personalized and direct communication with supporters.

- Effective for time-sensitive calls to action.

Disadvantages:

- Limited message length.
- Potential privacy concerns and compliance issues.

Technology for Achieving Desired Outcomes

Predictive Analytics Tools (e.g., IBM SPSS, SAS Analytics):

Advantages:

- Analyzes historical data to predict legislative outcomes.
- Identifies key influencers and likely supporters or opponents.
- Helps in crafting strategic interventions.

Disadvantages:

- Requires high-quality data for accurate predictions.
- Complex setup and interpretation requiring expert knowledge.

Lobbying CRM Systems (e.g., Quorum, Phone2Action):

Advantages:

- Centralizes all lobbying activities and interactions.
- Tracks legislator engagement and relationship history.
- Provides detailed reports and analytics on lobbying efforts.

Disadvantages:

- High cost of implementation and maintenance.

- Requires training for practical use.

Virtual Meeting and Collaboration Tools (e.g., Zoom, Microsoft Teams):

Advantages:

- Facilitates remote lobbying and stakeholder engagement.
- Provides tools for virtual presentations and collaborative document editing.
- Enhances communication with geographically dispersed supporters.

Disadvantages:

- Dependent on stable internet connections.
- Potential security concerns with sensitive information.

Using Technology to Motivate Proponents

Engagement Through Personalized Communication:

- Use customer relations management (CRM) systems to track supporter preferences and tailor messages accordingly.
- Deploy automated email campaigns with personalized content to maintain engagement.
- Utilize text messaging for direct and immediate communication, particularly for urgent calls to action.

Leveraging Social Media for Advocacy:

- Use social media monitoring tools to identify and engage with key influencers.

- Create compelling content that resonates with your audience and encourages them to act.
- Organize virtual events and live streams to discuss legislative issues and mobilize supporters.

Data-Driven Campaign Strategies:

- Employ predictive analytics to identify the most effective campaign strategies and messaging.
- Use data visualization tools to present clear and compelling arguments to supporters and legislators.
- Continuously analyze campaign data to refine and improve strategies.

Grassroots Mobilization:

- Utilize advocacy platforms to organize petition drives and grassroots campaigns.
- Engage supporters through social media and email to participate in rallies, town halls, and other events.
- Provide supporters with the tools and resources they need to advocate effectively on your behalf.

Case Studies: Successful Technology-Driven Lobbying Campaigns

Case Study 1

Mobilizing Healthcare Advocates with Predictive Analytics: A healthcare organization used predictive analytics to identify key legislative targets for a campaign to increase funding for rural health clinics. They secured additional funding by focusing their efforts on swing legislators identified through data analysis.

Case Study 2

Social Media Engagement in Charitable Gaming: An environmental group utilized social media monitoring tools to track public sentiment on a proposed climate bill. Engaging influencers and creating viral content mobilized significant public support, which pressured legislators to pass the bill.

Case Study 3

Virtual Lobbying for Education of Assisted Living Staff: An assisted living advocacy group used virtual meeting tools to lobby for increased funding for online learning resources. By organizing virtual town halls and meetings with legislators, they successfully influenced the passage of critical funding legislation.

Ethical Considerations and Best Practices

Respect for Privacy:

- Ensure compliance with data protection laws and regulations.
- Be transparent with supporters about how their data is collected and used.
- Implement robust security measures to protect sensitive information.

Transparency and Honesty:

- Communicate your goals and strategies to supporters and stakeholders.

- Avoid misleading or manipulative tactics in your campaigns.
- Provide accurate and truthful information to legislators and the public.

Accountability:

- Establish clear lines of accountability within your organization for the use of technology.
- Regularly review and audit your technology usage to ensure ethical practices.
- Be prepared to address any concerns or issues that arise promptly and transparently.

Incorporating modern technology into your legislative lobbying efforts can significantly enhance your ability to gather information, mobilize supporters, and achieve your desired outcomes. By leveraging advanced research tools, social media monitoring, predictive analytics, and personalized communication, you can create data-driven, effective campaigns that resonate with both legislators and the public.

However, it is essential to navigate the associated ethical considerations carefully and ensure transparency, accountability, and respect for privacy in all your efforts. As technology evolves, staying informed and adaptable will be key to maintaining a competitive edge in the legislative process.

"Using technology in a political campaign is like sending your grandma a text—you're not sure she'll get it, but when she does, she'll tell everyone she knows . . . twice."

— Unknown

Chapter 24: Implementing Technology on a Limited Budget

"Effective advocacy doesn't always require a big budget; it requires smart use of technology. With limited resources, you can leverage digital tools like social media, email campaigns, and online petitions to reach legislators and mobilize supporters without breaking the bank."

—*Stephanie Vance, from The Influence Game*

When I first started running campaigns, I assumed that using technology required a big budget and expensive tools. But over the years, I've learned that even with limited resources, you can still leverage technology to run an efficient and impactful campaign. It doesn't take a fortune to organize your efforts, spread your message, and engage with supporters. For example, free or low-cost tools like Google Workspace or Microsoft Excel can help you create databases to track supporters, monitor progress, and manage outreach. Social media platforms like Facebook, X, and Instagram are free and allow you to reach a large audience quickly with strategic posts, videos, or live events. I've also used affordable email platforms like Mailchimp to communicate with key stakeholders and keep everyone informed. With creativity and some strategic planning, technology becomes a powerful tool that's accessible to any campaign, no matter the budget.

What's important is focusing on the tools that will deliver the most value for your specific goals. You don't need every fancy app or expensive platform—just the ones that help you engage the right people and move your campaign forward. For instance, I've used free online petition platforms to show grassroots support for an issue, which gave legislators concrete evidence of voter interest. In another campaign, I used Zoom to host a series of virtual town halls, connecting constituents with lawmakers directly, all at minimal cost. The key is working smarter, not harder—using simple, effective tools that save time and amplify your efforts. In this chapter, I'll walk you through practical, budget-friendly ways to incorporate technology into your campaign, proving that you don't need a massive budget to deliver big results. It's about resourcefulness and making the most of what's already at your fingertips.

In this chapter you will learn about

- Social media advocacy.
- Email campaigns.
- Online petitions.
- Webinars and online meetings.
- Crowdfunding and donations.
- Volunteer management.
- Data management.
- Advocacy software.

- Partnerships and collaborations.
- Educational content and resources.

1. Social Media Advocacy

- **Platforms:** Utilize free social media platforms like Facebook, Twitter, Instagram, and LinkedIn.
- **Content Creation:** Create compelling and shareable content. Use infographics, short videos, and testimonials to engage your audience.
- **Scheduled Posts:** Schedule posts using free tools like Buffer or Hootsuite to maintain a consistent online presence.
- **Engagement:** Actively engage with your audience by responding to comments and messages and participating in relevant discussions and hashtags.

2. Email Campaigns

- **Email Marketing Services:** Use affordable or free tiers of email marketing services like Mailchimp or Sendinblue to manage and automate your email campaigns.
- **Targeted Emails:** Segment your email list to send targeted messages to different groups within your audience.
- **Newsletter:** Regularly send updates, calls to action, and educational content to keep your supporters informed and engaged.

3. Online Petitions

- **Petition Platforms:** Use free online petition platforms like Change.org or GoPetition to create and distribute petitions.
- **Promotion:** Promote the petition through social media channels, email lists, and website to gather signatures.

4. Webinars and Online Meetings

- **Video Conferencing Tools:** Use free or low-cost video conferencing tools like Zoom, Google Meet, or Microsoft Teams for webinars, town halls, and strategy meetings.
- **Event Promotion:** Promote these events via social media, email campaigns, and on your website.
- **Recording:** Record webinars and meetings to share with those who couldn't attend live.

5. Crowdfunding and Donations

- **Crowdfunding Platforms:** Use crowdfunding platforms like GoFundMe, Kickstarter, or Indiegogo to raise funds for your campaign.
- **Donation Buttons:** Use services like PayPal or Stripe to add donation buttons to your website and social media profiles.
- **Fundraising Events:** Host virtual fundraising events to engage supporters and solicit donations.

6. Volunteer Management

- **Volunteer Platforms:** Use platforms like Volunteer Match or Signup Genius to recruit and manage volunteers.
- **Task Management:** Use free project management tools like Trello or Asana to organize tasks and communicate with volunteers.

7. Data Management

- **CRM Tools:** Use affordable CRM tools, such as HubSpot's free tier or Zoho CRM, to manage supporter data and track interactions.
- **Data Analysis:** Use tools like Google Analytics and Facebook Insights to analyze your online engagement and adjust your strategy accordingly.

8. Advocacy Software

- **Affordable Solutions:** Look for affordable or nonprofit-discounted advocacy software like Nation Builder or Salsa Labs that offer comprehensive campaign management tools.
- **Grassroots Mobilization:** Use these tools to facilitate grassroots mobilization efforts, including phone banking, door-to-door canvassing, and letter-writing campaigns.

9. Partnerships and Collaborations

- **Network:** Partner with other organizations, coalitions, and influencers to amplify your message and resources.

- **Shared Resources:** Share resources, such as technology tools and volunteer networks, to reduce costs and increase efficiency.

10. Educational Content and Resources

- **DIY Resources:** Create and share DIY resources such as guides, templates, and toolkits to empower your supporters to act independently.
- **Online Libraries:** Develop a library of resources, including fact sheets, policy briefs, and talking points that supporters can access and use.

An association or business can effectively run a legislative campaign even on a limited budget by strategically using these affordable and accessible tools and platforms. Consistent engagement, and innovative use of technology to maximize impact without overspending.

Now, we will explore research sources that will provide you with all the information you need to effectively lobby your issue with the legislature. Remember, information is power, and knowing where to find it is critical to any successful campaign.

"Whoever would overthrow the liberty of a nation
must begin by subduing the freeness of speech."
— Benjamin Franklin

Chapter 25: Vital Information Sources Every Lobbyist Should Know

"To be effective, a lobbyist must master the art of information gathering. Understanding the nuances of legislative calendars, tracking bills, and knowing when and where decisions are made are essential tools that allow you to stay ahead and advocate effectively."

— *Paul A. Miller*

As a lobbyist, having access to a comprehensive range of information sources is essential to managing a client's legislative activities and achieving their goals. Early in my career, I thought simply reading bills, attending hearings, and using basic tracking tools would be enough to stay ahead. I quickly learned that the legislative process is far more complex and dynamic than it appears on the surface. Information is constantly changing, bills get amended, alliances shift, and priorities evolve overnight. To keep up, I rely on a variety of sources, including legislative databases, committee reports, fiscal notes, and public records, but that's just the starting point. I also monitor social media, press releases, and stakeholder publications to get a broader understanding of the public sentiment and political pressures shaping the debate. This layered approach ensures I'm not just reacting to events but staying proactive and well-prepared.

Equally important are the relationships I've built with key contacts over the years. Some of the most valuable insights come from direct conversations with legislative staff, agency officials, and even other lobbyists. I've had aides tip me off about amendments before they were filed, and I've gotten critical intel about the political dynamics surrounding a bill simply by taking the time to listen. These relationships allow me to gain firsthand information that isn't available in any database or report. However, these connections don't happen by accident. They require trust, credibility, and consistent effort to maintain. By combining robust information sources with strong personal relationships, I can ensure my clients are always informed, prepared, and positioned for success. In this chapter, we'll explore the essential tools and strategies you need to master the art of staying ahead in the legislative process.

In this chapter you will learn about

- Various information sources.
- The Legislative Information Portal
- Legislative archives.

Legislative Calendars

Sources: Legislative websites, committee-specific web pages, and government portals.

Usage: Track upcoming hearings, meetings, and deadlines for bills under consideration by various committees. Helps in planning attendance and participation.

> **Pro Tip:** Think of committee calendars like your daily planner. Keeping an eye on them ensures you get to all critical meetings and deadlines. During my years of lobbying, I learned an important lesson: always read the calendar. I didn't follow this practice religiously and realized I had a significant hearing the next day. I hadn't prepared; I was caught with my pants down. I spent the afternoon and evening preparing. Fortunately, I got the bill out of committee. But I almost bungled everything. READ THE CALENDAR!

Status Sheets

Sources: Legislative information systems, official state or federal legislative websites.

Usage: Monitor the status of specific bills and resolutions, including their legislative progress. This allows for timely updates to clients and strategic adjustments.

> **Pro Tip:** Status sheets are your report cards for bills. Regularly check them to gauge progress and plan your next moves.

House and Senate Calendars

Sources: Official House of Representatives and Senate websites, legislative tracking services.

Usage: Stay informed about the daily schedule of floor sessions, debates, and votes. It is essential to know when critical votes or discussions are occurring.

> **Pro Tip:** Treat these calendars like a TV guide for legislative sessions. Knowing the schedule helps you tune in at the correct time

Legislator Information

Sources: Legislative websites, legislators' websites, biographical directories, and social media profiles.

Usage: Gather background information on legislators, including their voting records, committee memberships, and policy interests. Helps tailor advocacy efforts and build relationships.

> **Pro Tip:** Consider this as creating a dating profile for each legislator. The more you know, the better you can tailor your approach.

Legislative Information Portals

Sources: Government portals like Congress.gov, state legislative websites, and specialized legislative tracking services.

Usage: Access comprehensive legislative databases for bill texts, summaries, amendments, voting records, and sponsor details. Provides a one-stop resource for all legislative information.

> **Pro Tip:** Use these portals as your legislative Swiss Army knife—everything you need in one place.

Government and Legislative Libraries

Sources: Library of Congress, state legislative libraries, and online legal research databases.

Usage: Conduct in-depth research on legislative history, legal precedents, and policy analyses. It is essential to prepare detailed briefs and understand the implications of legislation.

> **Pro Tip:** Treat these libraries like the ultimate reference section. They hold the depth of knowledge you need for thorough research.

Lobbying and Advocacy Organizations

Sources: National associations, advocacy groups, and think tanks.

Usage: Leverage these organizations' reports, position papers, and policy recommendations to support lobbying efforts. Often provide expert analyses and strategic insights.

> **Pro Tip:** Think of these organizations as your strategic allies. Their insights can bolster your position and provide new angles for your arguments.

News Media and Press Releases

Sources: Major news outlets, political news websites, and official press releases from legislative offices.

Usage: Stay updated on breaking news, political developments, and public statements from key legislators. This helps you stay ahead of the curve and respond quickly to new developments.

> **Pro Tip:** Use the media as your legislative radar. It helps you spot changes and developments before they occur.

Legislative Tracking Software

Sources: Tools like Colorado Capitol Watch, Quorum, Fiscal Note, and State Net.

Usage: Use advanced features like bill tracking, report generation, and stakeholder mapping to manage and streamline legislative activities. Provides real-time updates and alerts.

> **Pro Tip:** Think of this software as your legislative command center. It keeps all your information organized and accessible in real time.

Public Records and Transparency Websites

Sources: State and federal public records websites, transparency initiatives.

Usage: Access public records such as campaign finance reports, lobbying disclosures, and government contracts. This is important for understanding the broader context and potential influences on legislators.

> **Pro Tip:** Treat these records like magnifying glass. They help you see the hidden details influencing legislative actions.

Social Media and Online Forums

Sources: Twitter, Facebook, LinkedIn, and specialized political discussion forums.

Usage: Follow legislators, political commentators, and advocacy groups for real-time updates and informal insights. Engage in discussions and network with other professionals.

> *Pro Tip:* Use social media as your ear to the ground. It provides immediate insights and connects you with a broader community.

Policy Research Organizations

Sources: Nonprofit research organizations, academic institutions, and policy think tanks.

Usage: Utilize research reports, policy briefs, and statistical analyses to support evidence-based advocacy. Provides credibility and depth to lobbying efforts.

> *Pro Tip:* Think of these organizations as your legislative think tanks. Their detailed analyses add weight to your arguments.

Constituent Feedback and Grassroots Input

Sources: Surveys, town hall meetings, and grassroots advocacy platforms.

Usage: Gather and present constituent opinions and grassroots support to legislators. Demonstrates public backing and can influence legislative decisions.

> **Pro Tip:** Treat grassroots input like your barometer for public sentiment. It shows you where the winds of public opinion are blowing.

Historical Legislative Records

Sources: Archives of legislative bodies, historical societies, and digital archives.

Usage: Research the historical context and evolution of specific policies and legislative practices. Helps in crafting arguments based on historical precedents.

> **Pro Tip:** Use historical records as your time machine. Understanding the past can help you shape the future.

Professional Networks and Associations

Sources: Professional lobbying associations, legislative liaisons, and industry groups.

Usage: Network with other lobbyists and professionals to share information, strategies, and insights. Enhances collaborative efforts and knowledge sharing.

> **Pro Tip:** Think of professional networks as your legislative ecosystem. Collaboration and shared knowledge enhance your effectiveness.

Key Contacts for Firsthand Legislative Information

Building relationships with key contacts is crucial for gaining valuable firsthand information. These individuals can provide insights, early alerts, and nuanced understanding that public sources cannot.

1. Legislative Aides and Staffers

Role: These are the primary assistants to legislators and are often involved in drafting legislation, conducting research, and managing schedules.

Usage: Build relationships with aides and staffers to gain insights into legislative priorities, upcoming bills, and the nuances of the legislative process. They can provide early alerts on committee meetings and pending votes.

> *Pro Tip:* Treat legislative aides like the backstage crew in a theater. They know what's happening behind the scenes and can give you the inside scoop.

2. Committee Staff

Role: These individuals manage the administrative tasks for legislative committees, including scheduling hearings and maintaining records.

Usage: Contact committee clerks for information on committee agendas, witness lists, and procedural developments. They can offer updates on the status of bills within their committees.

> *Pro Tip:* Committee clerks are like the gatekeepers of the legislative process. Building a good rapport with them opens many doors.

3. Legislative Counsel

Role: Legislative counsel provides legal and technical advice to legislators and committees on bill drafting and legal implications.

Usage: Seek guidance from legislative counsels to understand the legal nuances and potential impacts of proposed legislation. They can also clarify the legislative language and procedural questions.

> **Pro Tip:** Think of legislative counsels as your legal navigators. They help you chart the course through complex legislative waters.

4. Lobbyists and Advocacy Group Representatives

Role: Fellow lobbyists and representatives from advocacy groups often have specialized knowledge and access to insider information.

Usage: Network with other lobbyists to share information, strategies, and insights. Building a coalition or partnership with aligned interests can strengthen your lobbying efforts.

> **Pro Tip:** Consider other lobbyists as your comrades in the trenches. Sharing information and strategies can lead to mutual success.

5. Journalists and Political Reporters

Role: Reporters covering the legislative beat often have deep networks within the government and early access to information.

Usage: Develop relationships with journalists to gain insights into political dynamics and upcoming legislative moves. They can provide context and background that may not be publicly available.

> **Pro Tip:** Treat journalists like your legislative watch-dogs. They often know about developments before they become public.

6. State Department Legislative Liaisons

Role: These officers represent various departments, agencies, or organizations and act as liaisons with the legislature.

Usage: Engage with government relations officers to get updates on administrative positions and actions related to specific legislation. They can offer perspectives on how executive agencies view pending bills.

> **Pro Tip:** Consider government relations officers as your diplomatic contacts. They provide valuable perspectives from the administrative side.

7. Leadership Staff

Role: Whips and leadership staff are crucial in managing party discipline and legislative strategy.

Usage: Connect with whips and leadership staff to understand party priorities and strategies. They can provide insights into which bills will likely move forward and how party members may vote.

> **Pro Tip:** Think of party whips as the legislative power brokers. They have the pulse on party strategy and can guide you accordingly.

8. Constituent Liaisons

Role: Constituent liaisons handle communications between legislators and their constituents.

Usage: Use information from constituent liaisons to understand the concerns and opinions of the legislator's voters. This can help in framing your advocacy messages to align with constituent interests.

> ⚖ ***Pro Tip:*** Treat constituent liaisons as your public opinion analysts. They know what issues are essential to the voters.

9. Policy Analysts and Researchers

Role: These individuals provide detailed analyses and reports on legislative issues and policy impacts.

Usage: Consult policy analysts for in-depth research and expert opinions on specific legislative matters. They can help bolster your arguments with data and well-founded analyses.

> ⚖ ***Pro Tip:*** Policy analysts are like your legislative detectives. They dig deep into the details to provide robust evidence.

10. Former Legislators and Retired Officials

Role: Individuals who previously served in the legislature often retain valuable knowledge and connections.

Usage: Seek advice and insights from former legislators and officials to understand historical contexts and procedural intricacies. Based on their experience, they can offer mentorship and strategic advice.

> ⚖ ***Pro Tip:*** Former legislators are like your wise elders. Their experience and knowledge can provide invaluable guidance.

Building and Leveraging Relationships

Regular Communication

Maintain regular, respectful communication with these contacts. Keep them updated on your interests and offer insights or information that might also be valuable to them.

Mutual Benefits

Focus on building mutually beneficial relationships. Offer support and assistance when appropriate and be a reliable source of information.

Confidentiality and Trust

Handle sensitive information with discretion to build trust. Demonstrating reliability and trustworthiness can lead to more open information sharing.

Active Participation

Attend legislative events, hearings, and networking functions to interact with these key individuals. Active participation helps build a visible presence and establish connections.

Follow-Up

Follow up with a thank-you note or email after meetings or discussions. Express appreciation for their time and information and keep the lines of communication open for future interactions.

> **Pro Tip:** Building relationships is like tending a garden. Regular care and attention yield the best results.

By effectively utilizing these extensive information sources and building strong relationships with key contacts, as a lobbyist you can stay well informed, strategically navigate the legislative process, and successfully manage your clients' legislative activities to achieve desired outcomes. Information is power in the legislative arena, and mastering the art of gathering and leveraging this information is essential for any successful lobbyist.

Remember, being a successful lobbyist is like being a master chess player. You must anticipate your opponent's moves, gather as much intelligence as possible, and strategically deploy your pieces to win the game. In the legislative arena, intelligence is your most powerful weapon.

There is a steady infringement on a lobbyist's ability to lobby the legislature. More and more rules are being adopted to curtail a lobbyist's ability to do his job on behalf of his client. There are pros and cons to this trend. We will explore them in the next chapter.

"Freedom is worth fighting for. We will stand firm in the face of threats to our liberty."

— Governor Ron DeSantis

Chapter 26: Lobbying in a Changing World

"In recent years, there has been a clear trend toward imposing stricter regulations on lobbyists, aiming to reduce their direct involvement in the legislative process. While well-intentioned, these restrictions often push lobbying behind closed doors, where transparency and accountability become more difficult to maintain."

— *Thomas E. Mann*

I n recent years, I've noticed a growing effort to regulate and limit lobbyists' involvement in the legislative process. These measures, often aimed at increasing transparency and reducing undue influence, are designed to ensure fairness and accountability in policymaking. While I understand the intentions behind them, these restrictions can create unintended roadblocks that ultimately weaken the legislative process. I've encountered situations where limitations on when and how lobbyists can engage with legislators prevented me from providing crucial information at a key moment. In one case, a regulation meant to curb lobbying during certain periods forced me to wait until a hearing was nearly over to address a major misunderstanding about my client's issue. By then, it was almost too late to fix the narrative, and the policy outcome suffered as a result. Ironically, such rules can reduce transparency by cutting off informed voices at critical stages of decision-making.

These regulations don't just create logistical challenges for lobbyists. They also have real consequences for public policy. Restricting access to lawmakers can mean less accountability, fewer informed perspectives, and more reliance on rushed or incomplete information. I've worked on complex issues where the technical details of a bill were misunderstood because rules prevented me from meeting with lawmakers at the right time. In one instance, a poorly worded amendment was passed because I couldn't explain its unintended consequences until after the fact, forcing the legislature to revisit the issue in the next session. Lobbyists provide expertise, represent diverse interests, and serve as a critical link between stakeholders and legislators. Overregulating our work, while well intentioned, risks creating a less informed and less accountable legislative process. In this chapter, we'll explore these trends in greater detail and discuss how we can strike a balance between promoting transparency and ensuring effective advocacy.

In this chapter you will learn about

- Registration requirements.
- What you can and cannot do with legislators.
- Restriction of lobbying expenses.
- Limits on campaign contributions.

1. Registration and Disclosure Requirements

Description: Lobbyists must register with government agencies and disclose their clients, the issues they are lobbying on, and the amount of money spent on lobbying activities.

Limitations:

- **Transparency vs. Privacy:** Lobbyists must disclose detailed information about their activities, which can limit their ability to operate discreetly.
- **Administrative Burden:** The need to regularly update and file reports adds an administrative burden, consuming time and resources that could be spent on advocacy.
- **Public Scrutiny:** Increased transparency leads to greater public and media scrutiny, which can impact a lobbyist's reputation and effectiveness.

2. Gift and Entertainment Bans

Description: Regulations often prohibit lobbyists from giving legislators and their staff gifts, meals, or entertainment to prevent undue influence.

Limitations:

- **Relationship Building:** These bans hinder lobbyists' ability to build personal relationships with legislators, which are crucial for effective advocacy.
- **Networking Opportunities:** Limits on social interactions reduce opportunities for informal networking and information exchange.

- **Increased Formality:** Lobbyists must rely on more formal and often less effective methods of communication.

3. Cooling-Off Periods

Description: Cooling-off periods require former legislators and government officials to wait for a specified period before they can engage in lobbying activities.

Limitations:

- **Loss of Expertise:** Former officials' immediate lobbying is restricted, temporarily reducing their expertise and insights into advocacy efforts.
- **Delays in Strategy:** Lobbying firms may face delays in executing strategies that rely on hiring experienced former officials.

4. Restrictions on Lobbying Expenditures

Description: Laws may limit the amount of money spent on lobbying activities or require detailed accounting of lobbying expenses.

Limitations:

- **Resource Allocation:** Lobbying firms must carefully allocate their resources, potentially limiting the scope and scale of their advocacy campaigns.
- **Financial Strain:** Smaller lobbying firms or those representing fewer wealthy clients may struggle to compete with better-funded interests.

- **Detailed Reporting:** The need for detailed financial reporting increases administrative overhead.

5. Limits on Campaign Contributions

Description: Regulations often cap the amount lobbyists can contribute to political campaigns or restrict contributions during legislative sessions.

Limitations:

- **Influence Reduction:** Limits on campaign contributions reduce a lobbyist's ability to gain access with legislators through financial support.
- **Strategic Constraints:** Lobbyists must find alternative strategies to support their allies in government.

6. Prohibition of Contingency Fees

Description: Many jurisdictions prohibit lobbyists from working on a contingency fee basis, where they are paid based on the success of their lobbying efforts.

Limitations:

- **Risk Management:** Lobbyists must assume financial risk regardless of the outcome, which could potentially reduce their willingness to take on challenging issues.
- **Payment Structures:** Lobbyists must negotiate different payment structures, which may be less appealing to clients.

7. Enhanced Reporting of Contacts

Description: Lobbyists must report all contacts with legislators and their staff, including discussed topics.

Limitations:

- **Privacy Concerns:** Detailed reporting of contacts can invade the privacy of both lobbyists and legislators.
- **Reduced Spontaneity:** The need to report every interaction can discourage spontaneous and informal discussions, limiting the flow of information.
- **Administrative Load:** Tracking and reporting every contact adds significant administrative work.

8. Ethics Training and Compliance Programs

Description: Lobbyists must often undergo ethics training and adhere to strict compliance programs.

Limitations:

- **Time and Resources:** Compliance programs and training sessions require time and resources that could be used for lobbying activities.
- **Increased Accountability:** Lobbyists are held to higher accountability standards, which can limit their flexibility and strategic options.

Impact on Lobbying Effectiveness

The increasing regulation of lobbying activities has both positive and negative impacts:

Positive Impacts:

- **Transparency and Trust:** Increased transparency can build public trust in the legislative process.
- **Ethical Standards:** Higher ethical standards help prevent corruption and ensure that lobbying is conducted fairly.

Negative Impacts:

- **Reduced Influence:** Regulations limit lobbyists' traditional methods to build relationships and influence legislation.
- **Increased Costs:** Compliance with regulations increases the cost of lobbying, potentially marginalizing smaller firms and less wealthy clients.
- **Operational Challenges:** Administrative burdens and inter-action restrictions can slow the advocacy process and reduce effectiveness.

As regulations evolve, lobbyists must adapt to new constraints while finding innovative ways to advocate effectively within the legal framework. Understanding these regulations and their limitations is crucial for navigating the increasingly complex landscape of legislative advocacy.

The Harmful Impact of Limiting Lobbyist-Elected Official Interactions

The trend toward increasing regulation of lobbying activities, while intended to promote transparency and reduce undue influence, has significant downsides for lobbyists and elected officials. By limiting interactions between these parties, these regulations can inadvertently harm the legislative process and the development of meaningful public policy.

For Lobbyists

Diminished Relationship Building

- **Impersonal Advocacy:** Lobbyists build personal relationships with elected officials to communicate their clients' positions and nuances effectively. Restrictions on gifts, meals, and social interactions make establishing the trust and rapport necessary for effective advocacy harder.
- **Reduced Influence:** The inability to engage in informal settings limits a lobbyist's ability to influence lawmakers. Personal connections often lead to more open and honest conversations, crucial for understanding and influencing legislative perspectives.

Increased Operational Costs

- **Administrative Burden:** Enhanced reporting and disclosure requirements add significant administrative overhead, diverting resources from strategic advocacy efforts.
- **Compliance Costs:** Adhering to complex regulations requires investing in legal and compliance resources, increasing operational costs, particularly for smaller lobbying firms and grassroots organizations.

Strategic Limitations

- **Loss of Flexibility:** Strict regulations and the need to disclose all interactions create a more rigid and less dynamic advocacy environment. Lobbyists lose the ability to react swiftly to changing legislative landscapes.

- **Cooling-Off Periods:** These periods delay the involvement of experienced former officials in lobbying efforts, depriving firms of valuable expertise and strategic insights.

For Elected Officials

Information Deficit

- **Reduced Access to Expertise:** Elected officials often rely on lobbyists for detailed information and expert insights on complex issues. Limiting interactions reduces the flow of critical information that can aid in informed decision-making.
- **One-Sided Perspectives:** Restrictions on lobbying can lead to an over-reliance on internal staff or select sources, potentially resulting in a less comprehensive understanding of issues.

Decreased Responsiveness

- **Less Feedback:** Regular, informal lobbyist interactions provide real-time feedback on proposed legislation. Without these interactions, legislators may miss out on immediate responses from various stakeholders, slowing the legislative process.
- **Diminished Dialogue:** Effective policymaking often involves back-and-forth discussions and negotiations. Restrictions can reduce opportunities for such dialogues, leading to less collaborative and more fragmented policymaking.

Impact on Public Policy

Quality of Legislation

- **Incomplete Information:** When elected officials lack access to the detailed and nuanced information provided by lobbyists, the quality of legislation can suffer. Policies may be based on incomplete or outdated information, leading to ineffective or poorly targeted laws.

- **Overly Cautious Policy:** Fear of public scrutiny and the risk of violating lobbying regulations can make officials and lobbyists overly cautious, leading to more conservative and less innovative policy solutions.

Public Engagement

- **Reduced Citizen Representation:** Lobbyists often represent diverse groups, including nonprofits, small businesses, and grassroots organizations. Increased regulations can disproportionately affect these groups, reducing their ability to influence policy and weakening democratic representation.

- **Transparency Paradox:** While the intention behind the regulation is to increase transparency, it can create a paradox where critical discussions move out of the public eye to avoid scrutiny, leading to less transparency in the decision-making process.

Policy Delay and Stagnation

- **Slower Legislative Process:** Increased reporting requirements and limited interactions can slow the legislative process, causing delays in addressing urgent issues.

- **Stagnant Policy Development:** A more restricted advocacy environment can lead to policy stagnation, as fewer innovative ideas and perspectives are brought to the table.

While lobbying regulations are designed to prevent corruption and ensure fairness, they also create significant barriers to effective advocacy and policymaking. The limitations on interactions between lobbyists and elected officials can lead to a less informed, less responsive, and more cautious legislative process. Ultimately, these constraints can hinder the development of meaningful public policy that accurately reflects and addresses the needs of diverse stakeholders. Balancing transparency and ethical standards with the need for open dialogue and effective advocacy is crucial for the health of the legislative process and the quality of public policy.

The administrative state is slowly eroding and usurping the legislature's power. In the next chapter, we will explore this in detail. The consequences are substantial.

"Politics is the only job where you can spend half your time raising money to keep your job, and the other half explaining why you're not doing it."

— Unknown

Chapter 27: The Administrative State

"The administrative state has grown to the point where much of the law governing daily life is made by administrative agencies rather than elected representatives. This shift in power raises serious concerns about accountability and the rule of law in making public policy."

—*Philip Hamburger*

The administrative state plays a critical role in enacting and enforcing public policy as created by legislation passed by the legislature. Essentially, its function is to implement legislative mandates and evaluate the outcomes of these actions. This involves interpreting statutes, issuing regulations, and ensuring compliance with the law.

Historically, the Chevron decision (*Chevron U.S.A., Inc. v. Natural Resources Defense Council, Inc.*, 1984) significantly impacted regulatory bodies. The Supreme Court ruled that when a statute is ambiguous, courts should defer to the interpretation of the agency charged with enforcing that statute, provided the interpretation is reasonable.

This principle, known as Chevron deference, allowed agencies considerable leeway in interpreting and implementing laws usually left for the legislature to decide.

Effects of the Chevron Decision

- **Enhanced Agency Authority:** Chevron's deference effectively expanded the power of regulatory agencies. They were given the autonomy to interpret ambiguous statutory language without extensive judicial interference, which allowed them to adapt and apply regulations flexibly and responsively to evolving circumstances.

- **Streamlined Policy Implementation:** Agencies could implement and enforce policies more efficiently as they didn't constantly need to seek judicial approval for their interpretations. This streamlined the regulatory process and enabled quicker responses to new challenges.

- **Judicial Efficiency:** Chevron's deference reduced the burden on courts to interpret complex and technical statutory language, especially in areas where agencies had specialized expertise. Courts could focus on broader legal principles rather than intricate details of regulatory interpretation.

Recent Supreme Court Ruling Impacting Chevron Deference

Recently, the Supreme Court has shifted away from the principles established in the Chevron decision. The Court's ruling in the case of *Kisor v. Wilkie* (2019) revisited the deference given to administrative agencies. While Kisor primarily focused on Auer deference (related to agency interpretations of their regulations), it signaled a broader reconsideration of judicial deference to agencies. Furthermore, the case of *West Virginia v. EPA* (2022) further curtailed agency power, emphasizing that significant policy decisions with vast economic and political implications require clear congressional authorization.

Implications of the Recent Rulings

- **Increased Judicial Scrutiny:** Agencies may now face more rigorous judicial scrutiny when interpreting statutes. Courts are less likely to defer to agency interpretations, particularly on significant issues, automatically, which could lead to more frequent challenges to agency actions and interpretations.

- **Requirement for Clear Congressional Authorization:** The recent rulings underscore the need for clear and explicit legislative mandates. Agencies must ensure that their actions are directly supported by clear statutory language, especially when dealing with substantial economic or political matters.

- **Potential Slowing of Regulatory Processes:** With increased judicial scrutiny and the need for explicit congressional authorization, the regulatory process may become slower and more cumbersome. Agencies might need more explicit legislative backing before enacting significant regulations, which could delay policy implementation.

- **Shift in Power Dynamics:** These rulings potentially shift power back towards the judiciary and the legislature, reducing the autonomous regulatory authority of administrative agencies. This may lead to a more balanced oversight mechanism and politicize regulatory actions as they become more directly tied to legislative intent.

While the Administrative State is pivotal in implementing legislative mandates and shaping public policy, recent Supreme Court rulings have significantly altered the landscape established by the Chevron decision. Agencies now operate under a framework that demands clearer legislative guidance and face greater judicial oversight, marking a notable shift in the balance of power between the branches of government in the regulatory process.

In a democratic society, citizen participation isn't just a right—it's an obligation. In the next chapter, we'll explore why active involvement is fundamental to democracy, building on the insights from the previous chapter. Democracy thrives when citizens are engaged, informed, and actively shape the policies that affect them. Understanding why participation is required is crucial to ensuring that government remains accountable and reflective of the people it serves.

"Democracy is the worst form of government, except for all those other forms that have been tried from time to time."

— Winston Churchill

Chapter 28: Active Citizenship

"Democracy doesn't come from the top. It comes from the bottom. Democracy is not what governments do; its what people do. The government may try to limit public policy to what serves the interests of a few, but it is the job of citizens to ensure that public policy serves the interest of all."

—Howard Zinn, from
"A Power Governments Cannot Suppress."

As we conclude this comprehensive exploration of the legislative process, lobbying, and the regulations shaping these activities, it is crucial to emphasize the foundational principle that underpins a vibrant, accessible, and democratic society: active citizen participation.

Review and Synthesis

Throughout the previous chapters, we have detailed the intricacies of the legislative process, the essential role lobbyists play in informing and influencing policy, the impact of regulations on their work, and the evolving landscape of legislative advocacy. We have explored how lobbyists, when operating within ethical boundaries, can enhance the legislative process by providing valuable information, representing diverse interests, increasing citizen involvement and facilitating dialogue between constituents and lawmakers.

However, as regulations increasingly limit these interactions, the burden falls even more heavily on individual citizens to step up and engage actively in the democratic process. The health of our democracy depends not only on the transparency and fairness of the legislative process but also on the active involvement of its citizens.

The Vital Role of Citizen Participation

Citizen participation is the bedrock of a functioning democracy. When citizens are informed, engaged, and active, they ensure their voices are heard and their interests are represented. This participation can take many forms, including voting, attending town hall meetings, engaging in public discourse, joining advocacy groups, and contacting elected officials.

Key Benefits of Active Participation:

- Representation: Ensures that diverse voices and perspectives are considered in policymaking.
- Accountability: Holds elected officials and institutions accountable for their actions and decisions.
- Empowerment: Empowers individuals to influence the direction of their community and country.

The Consequences of Diminished Participation

1. Weakening of Democratic Institutions

Without active citizen involvement, democratic institutions become vulnerable to influence by a few powerful interests, undermining their representativeness and accountability.

2. Loss of Personal Freedoms

A disengaged citizenry leads to a concentration of power in the hands of a few. This imbalance can erode personal freedoms as policies may become skewed to favor narrow interests rather than the common good.

3. Deterioration of Public Policy

Public policies are most effective when they are informed by a broad spectrum of perspectives and experiences. Diminished citizen participation leads to a lack of diversity in viewpoints, resulting in less comprehensive and less effective policy decisions.

4. Erosion of Public Trust

When citizens feel they are not a part of the legislative process, trust in government declines. This can lead to apathy, cynicism, and further disengagement, creating a vicious cycle that weakens the fabric of society.

> **Pro Tip:** Think of citizen participation as the immune system of democracy. When it's strong, it fights off threats and keeps the body politic healthy.

The Call to Action

The active involvement of its citizens sustains a free society. When citizens participate in the democratic process, personal freedoms and the community's collective well-being are protected and enhanced. Individuals must recognize their role and responsibility in shaping the laws and policies that govern them.

Steps for Effective Participation:

1. Stay Informed

Keep abreast of current events, understand the issues at stake, and educate yourself about the legislative process. Subscribe to reliable news sources, follow legislative updates, and engage in discussions to broaden your understanding.

> *Pro Tip:* Staying informed is like keeping your GPS updated. It ensures you're always on the right track and can navigate the complexities of political landscapes.

2. Engage with Elected Officials

Reach out to your elected officials to express your views, ask questions, and provide input on legislative matters. Attending town hall meetings, write letters, and schedule meetings with your representatives.

> *Pro Tip:* Engaging with legislators is like coaching a sports team. Provide feedback, encouragement, and strategies to help them better represent you. You elected them, make them work for you.

3. Join Advocacy Groups

Become involved with organizations that represent your interests and values. These groups can amplify your voice and provide a platform for collective action. Join local chapters, participate in events, and contribute to their initiatives.

> **Pro Tip:** Joining advocacy groups is like joining a band. Together, you create a powerful symphony that resonates with policymakers.

4. Vote

Exercise your right to vote in all elections, from local to national. Your vote is a powerful tool for shaping the direction of your community and country. Research candidates and issues thoroughly before casting your ballot.

> **Pro Tip:** Voting is like planting a tree. It may seem small at first, but it grows into a mighty force for change over time.

5. Encourage Others

Foster a culture of participation by encouraging family, friends, and colleagues to engage in the democratic process. Share information, discuss issues, and motivate others to take action.

> **Pro Tip:** Encouraging others to participate is like starting a dance. Once a few people join in, it becomes a lively and impactful movement.

The Strength of Collective Action

When citizens come together, they can achieve remarkable things. History is replete with examples of grassroots movements that have brought about significant change. The civil rights movement, women's suffrage, environmental activism, and many other causes succeeded because ordinary people decided to act.

Building Momentum

Change often starts with a small group of committed individuals. By joining forces with like-minded people, you can build momentum and create a ripple effect that leads to substantial societal changes.

> **Pro Tip:** Think of building momentum like rolling a snowball down a hill. It starts small but grows more significant and more powerful as it gathers support.

Leveraging Technology

In today's digital age, technology offers powerful tools for civic engagement. Social media platforms, online petitions, and digital advocacy campaigns can mobilize people quickly and efficiently.

> **Pro Tip:** Use technology like a megaphone. It amplifies your voice and helps you reach a broader audience.

The Role of Education

Education plays a critical role in fostering active citizenship. By understanding the legislative process, the role of lobbyists, and the impact of public policy, citizens are better equipped to engage effectively.

> **Pro Tip:** Treat education like the foundation of a house. A solid understanding of the political system supports all your advocacy efforts. Civics education needs to be reintroduced in our education system. Freedom can only be assured through an educated public.

The Future of Citizen Participation

As we look to the future, citizen participation in democracy will only become more critical. Emerging technologies, changing demographics, and evolving political landscapes will present new challenges and opportunities for engagement. As a lobbyist you are there to encourage their involvement.

Embracing Innovation

Innovative tools and platforms will continue transforming citizens' engagement with the political process. Virtual town halls, online voting, and digital forums will make participation more accessible and convenient.

> **Pro Tip:** Embrace innovation like a new gadget. It may take some time, but it can make your life much easier.

Fostering Inclusivity

Ensuring that all voices are heard, particularly those of marginalized communities, will be essential for a healthy democracy. Efforts to increase inclusivity and representation must be prioritized.

> **Pro Tip:** Foster inclusivity by adding diverse ingredients to a recipe. This enriches the flavor and makes the final dish more delicious for everyone.

Strengthening Civic Education

Investing in civic education will empower the next generation of citizens to participate effectively in the democratic process. Schools, community organizations, and media outlets all have roles to play in this effort.

> **Pro Tip:** Treat civic education like planting seeds in a garden. With care and attention, it will grow into a flourishing landscape of informed and active citizens.

The strength and resilience of a democratic society are rooted in the active participation of its citizens. As we have explored throughout this book, the legislative process is complex and multifaceted, involving many players and interests. While lobbyists play a crucial role, their influence is tempered by regulations that ensure fairness and transparency.

Ultimately, every citizen is responsible for engaging in this process and ensuring that the laws and policies enacted reflect the collective will and serve the common good. A free society is diminished without citizen participation, and personal freedoms are at risk of being lost. Therefore, let us commit to active participation in our democracy, protecting and strengthening the foundations of our free and democratic society.

Call to Action:

- Stay Informed: Make it a habit to stay updated on political and legislative developments.
- Engage Actively: Reach out to your representatives, join advocacy groups, and participate in public discourse.
- Vote: Never underestimate the power of your vote.

- Encourage Others: Spread the word and motivate others to participate.

Remember, democracy is not a spectator sport. It requires all of us to get involved, stay engaged, and work together to shape a better future. So, roll up your sleeves, join the conversation, and make your voice heard. Together, we can ensure that our democracy remains strong, vibrant, and truly representative of the people it serves.

> "Nobody will ever deprive the American people of the right to vote except the American people themselves, and the only way they could do this is by not voting."
>
> — Franklin D. Roosevelt

Chapter 29: **Turning Strategy into Success**

I n *Hardball Advocacy: Secrets of the Lobby*, we've journeyed through the complex and dynamic world of professional lobbying. We started by exploring the foundational tools that every successful lobbyist must have, from strategic planning to relationship-building. We discussed the importance of clear communication with legislators, regulators, and staff and how to effectively navigate the media landscape to shape public opinion.

We delved into the art of understanding your opposition—knowing their motives, strategies, and plans—so you can stay one step ahead. We explored how lobbyists adapt in an ever-changing world, where regulations and limits on involvement constantly shift. We also examined the role of citizen participation in democracy, reminding us that lobbying is not just about advancing a single agenda but also about ensuring the legislative process remains responsive to the voices of the people.

Through case studies, personal stories, and strategic insights, this book has provided a comprehensive guide to mastering the art of lobbying. It's a profession that requires resilience, creativity, and the ability to play the game of influence with precision. As you move forward, remember that the true power of advocacy lies in understanding the system, building strong relationships, and never underestimating the impact of persistence.

The strategies shared in these chapters are designed to help you navigate the challenges and seize the opportunities in the world of public policy. The secrets of the lobby are now in your hands—it's up to you to apply them and shape the future of the causes you represent and support.

The United States Constitution

We the People of the United States, in Order to form a more perfect Union, establish Justice, insure domestic Tranquility, provide for the common defence, promote the general Welfare, and secure the Blessings of Liberty to ourselves and our Posterity, do ordain and establish this Constitution for the United States of America.

The Constitutional Convention

Article I

Section 1: Congress

All legislative Powers herein granted shall be vested in a Congress of the United States, which shall consist of a Senate and House of Representatives.

Section 2: The House of Representatives

The House of Representatives shall be composed of Members chosen every second Year by the People of the several States, and the Electors in each State shall have the Qualifications requisite for Electors of the most numerous Branch of the State Legislature.

No Person shall be a Representative who shall not have attained to the Age of twenty five Years, and been seven Years a Citizen of the United States, and who shall not, when elected, be an Inhabitant of that State in which he shall be chosen.

Representatives and direct Taxes shall be apportioned among the several States which may be included within this Union, according to their respective Numbers, which shall be determined by adding to the whole Number of free Persons, including those bound to Service for a Term of Years, and excluding Indians not taxed, three fifths of all other Persons. The actual Enumeration shall be made within three Years after the first Meeting of the Congress of the United States, and within every subsequent Term of ten Years, in such Manner as they shall by Law direct. The Number of Representatives shall not exceed one for every thirty Thousand, but each State shall have at Least one Representative; and until such enumeration shall be made, the State of New Hampshire shall be entitled to chuse three, Massachusetts eight, Rhode-Island and Providence Plantations one, Connecticut five, New-York six, New Jersey four, Pennsylvania eight, Delaware one, Maryland six, Virginia ten, North Carolina five, South Carolina five, and Georgia three.

When vacancies happen in the Representation from any State, the Executive Authority thereof shall issue Writs of Election to fill such Vacancies.

The House of Representatives shall chuse their Speaker and other Officers; and shall have the sole Power of Impeachment.

Section 3: The Senate

The Senate of the United States shall be composed of two Senators from each State, chosen by the Legislature thereof, for six Years; and each Senator shall have one Vote.

Immediately after they shall be assembled in Consequence of the first Election, they shall be divided as equally as may be into three Classes. The Seats of the Senators of the first Class shall be vacated at the Expiration of the second Year, of the second Class at the Expiration of the fourth Year, and of the third Class at the Expiration of the sixth Year, so that one third may be chosen every second Year; and if Vacancies happen by Resignation, or otherwise, during the Recess of the Legislature of any State, the Executive thereof may make temporary Appointments until the next Meeting of the Legislature, which shall then fill such Vacancies.

No Person shall be a Senator who shall not have attained to the Age of thirty Years, and been nine Years a Citizen of the United States, and who shall not, when elected, be an Inhabitant of that State for which he shall be chosen.

The Vice President of the United States shall be President of the Senate, but shall have no Vote, unless they be equally divided.

The Senate shall chuse their other Officers, and also a President pro tempore, in the Absence of the Vice President, or when he shall exercise the Office of President of the United States.

The Senate shall have the sole Power to try all Impeachments. When sitting for that Purpose, they shall be on Oath or Affirmation. When the President of the United States is tried, the Chief Justice shall preside: And no Person shall be convicted without the Concurrence of two thirds of the Members present.

Judgment in Cases of Impeachment shall not extend further than to removal from Office, and disqualification to hold and enjoy any Office of honor, Trust or Profit under the United States: but the Party convicted shall nevertheless be liable and subject to Indictment, Trial, Judgment and Punishment, according to Law.

Section 4: Elections

The Times, Places and Manner of holding Elections for Senators and Representatives, shall be prescribed in each State by the Legislature thereof; but the Congress may at any time by Law make or alter such Regulations, except as to the Places of chusing Senators.

The Congress shall assemble at least once in every Year, and such Meeting shall be on the first Monday in December, unless they shall by Law appoint a different Day.

Section 5: Powers and Duties of Congress

Each House shall be the Judge of the Elections, Returns and Qualifications of its own Members, and a Majority of each shall constitute a Quorum to do Business; but a smaller Number may adjourn from day to day, and may be authorized to compel the Attendance of absent Members, in such Manner, and under such Penalties as each House may provide.

Each House may determine the Rules of its Proceedings, punish its Members for disorderly Behaviour, and, with the Concurrence of two thirds, expel a Member.

Each House shall keep a Journal of its Proceedings, and from time to time publish the same, excepting such Parts as may in their Judgment require Secrecy; and the Yeas and Nays of the Members of either House on any question shall, at the Desire of one fifth of those Present, be entered on the Journal.

Neither House, during the Session of Congress, shall, without the Consent of the other, adjourn for more than three days, nor to any other Place than that in which the two Houses shall be sitting.

Section 6: Rights and Disabilities of Members

The Senators and Representatives shall receive a Compensation for their Services, to be ascertained by Law, and paid out of the Treasury of the United States. They shall in all Cases, except Treason, Felony and Breach of the Peace, be privileged from Arrest during their Attendance at the Session of their respective Houses, and in going to and returning from the same; and for any Speech or Debate in either House, they shall not be questioned in any other Place.

No Senator or Representative shall, during the Time for which he was elected, be appointed to any civil Office under the Authority of the United States, which shall have been created, or the Emoluments whereof shall have been encreased during such time; and no Person holding any Office under the United States, shall be a Member of either House during his Continuance in Office.

Section 7: Legislative Process

All Bills for raising Revenue shall originate in the House of Representatives; but the Senate may propose or concur with Amendments as on other Bills.

Every Bill which shall have passed the House of Representatives and the Senate, shall, before it become a Law, be presented to the President of the United States; If he approve he shall sign it, but if not he shall return it, with his Objections to that House in which it shall have originated, who shall enter the Objections at large on their Journal, and proceed to reconsider it. If after such Reconsideration two thirds of that House shall agree to pass the Bill, it shall be sent, together with the Objections, to the other House, by which it shall likewise be reconsidered, and if approved by two thirds of that House, it shall become a Law. But in all such Cases the Votes of both Houses shall be determined by yeas and Nays, and the Names of the Persons voting for and against the Bill shall be entered on the Journal of each House respectively. If any Bill shall not be returned by the President within ten Days (Sundays excepted) after it shall have been presented to him, the Same shall be a Law, in like Manner as if he had signed it, unless the Congress by their Adjournment prevent its Return, in which Case it shall not be a Law.

Every Order, Resolution, or Vote to which the Concurrence of the Senate and House of Representatives may be necessary (except on a question of Adjournment) shall be presented to the President of the United States; and before the Same shall take Effect, shall be approved by him, or being disapproved by him, shall be repassed by two thirds of the Senate and House of Representatives, according to the Rules and Limitations prescribed in the Case of a Bill.

Section 8: Powers of Congress

The Congress shall have Power To lay and collect Taxes, Duties, Imposts and Excises, to pay the Debts and provide for the common Defence and general Welfare of the United States; but all Duties, Imposts and Excises shall be uniform throughout the United States;

To borrow Money on the credit of the United States;

To regulate Commerce with foreign Nations, and among the several States, and with the Indian Tribes;

To establish a uniform Rule of Naturalization, and uniform Laws on the subject of Bankruptcies throughout the United States;

To coin Money, regulate the Value thereof, and of foreign Coin, and fix the Standard of Weights and Measures;

To provide for the Punishment of counterfeiting the Securities and current Coin of the United States;

To establish Post Offices and post Roads;

To promote the Progress of Science and useful Arts, by securing for limited Times to Authors and Inventors the exclusive Right to their respective Writings and Discoveries;

To constitute Tribunals inferior to the supreme Court;

To define and punish Piracies and Felonies committed on the high Seas, and Offences against the Law of Nations;

To declare War, grant Letters of Marque and Reprisal, and make Rules concerning Captures on Land and Water;

To raise and support Armies, but no Appropriation of Money to that Use shall be for a longer Term than two Years;

To provide and maintain a Navy;

To make Rules for the Government and Regulation of the land and naval Forces;

To provide for calling forth the Militia to execute the Laws of the Union, suppress Insurrections and repel Invasions;

To provide for organizing, arming, and disciplining, the Militia, and for governing such Part of them as may be employed in the Service of the United States, reserving to the States respectively, the Appointment of the Officers, and the Authority of training the Militia according to the discipline prescribed by Congress;

To exercise exclusive Legislation in all Cases whatsoever, over such District (not exceeding ten Miles square) as may, by Cession of particular States, and the Acceptance of Congress, become the Seat of the Government of the United States, and to exercise like Authority over all Places purchased by the Consent of the Legislature of the State in which the Same shall be, for the Erection of Forts, Magazines, Arsenals, dock-Yards and other needful Buildings;-And

To make all Laws which shall be necessary and proper for carrying into Execution the foregoing Powers, and all other Powers vested by this Constitution in the Government of the United States, or in any Department or Officer thereof.

Section 9: Powers Denied Congress

The Migration or Importation of such Persons as any of the States now existing shall think proper to admit, shall not be prohibited by the Congress prior to the Year one thousand eight hundred and eight, but a Tax or duty may be imposed on such Importation, not exceeding ten dollars for each Person.

The Privilege of the Writ of Habeas Corpus shall not be suspended, unless when in Cases of Rebellion or Invasion the public Safety may require it.

No Bill of Attainder or ex post facto Law shall be passed.

No Capitation, or other direct, Tax shall be laid, unless in Proportion to the Census or enumeration herein before directed to be taken.

No Tax or Duty shall be laid on Articles exported from any State.

No Preference shall be given by any Regulation of Commerce or Revenue to the Ports of one State over those of another: nor shall Vessels bound to, or from, one State, be obliged to enter, clear, or pay Duties in another.

No Money shall be drawn from the Treasury, but in Consequence of Appropriations made by Law; and a regular Statement and Account of the Receipts and Expenditures of all public Money shall be published from time to time.

No Title of Nobility shall be granted by the United States: And no Person holding any Office of Profit or Trust under them, shall, without the Consent of the Congress, accept of any present, Emolument, Office, or Title, of any kind whatever, from any King, Prince, or foreign State.

Section 10: Powers Denied to the States

No State shall enter into any Treaty, Alliance, or Confederation; grant Letters of Marque and Reprisal; coin Money; emit Bills of Credit; make any Thing but gold and silver Coin a Tender in Payment of Debts; pass any Bill of Attainder, ex post facto Law, or Law impairing the Obligation of Contracts, or grant any Title of Nobility.

No State shall, without the Consent of the Congress, lay any Imposts or Duties on Imports or Exports, except what may be absolutely necessary for executing it's inspection Laws: and the net Produce of all Duties and Imposts, laid by any State on Imports or Exports, shall be for the Use of the Treasury of the United States; and all such Laws shall be subject to the Revision and Controul of the Congress.

No State shall, without the Consent of Congress, lay any Duty of Tonnage, keep Troops, or Ships of War in time of Peace, enter into any Agreement or Compact with another State, or with a foreign Power, or engage in War, unless actually invaded, or in such imminent Danger as will not admit of delay.

Article II

Section 1

The executive Power shall be vested in a President of the United States of America.

He shall hold his Office during the Term of four Years, and, together with the Vice President, chosen for the same Term, be elected, as follows:

Each State shall appoint, in such Manner as the Legislature thereof may direct, a Number of Electors, equal to the whole Number of Senators and Representatives to which the State may be entitled in the Congress: but no Senator or Representative, or Person holding an

Office of Trust or Profit under the United States, shall be appointed an Elector.

The Electors shall meet in their respective States, and vote by Ballot for two Persons, of whom one at least shall not be an Inhabitant of the same State with themselves. And they shall make a List of all the Persons voted for, and of the Number of Votes for each; which List they shall sign and certify, and transmit sealed to the Seat of the Government of the United States, directed to the President of the Senate. The President of the Senate shall, in the Presence of the Senate and House of Representatives, open all the Certificates, and the Votes shall then be counted. The Person having the greatest Number of Votes shall be the President, if such Number be a Majority of the whole Number of Electors appointed; and if there be more than one who have such Majority, and have an equal Number of Votes, then the House of Representatives shall immediately chuse by Ballot one of them for President; and if no Person have a Majority, then from the five highest on the List the said House shall in like Manner chuse the President. But in chusing the President, the Votes shall be taken by States, the Representation from each State having one Vote; A quorum for this Purpose shall consist of a Member or Members from two thirds of the States, and a Majority of all the States shall be necessary to a Choice. In every Case, after the Choice of the President, the Person having the greatest Number of Votes of the Electors shall be the Vice President. But if there should remain two or more who have equal Votes, the Senate shall chuse from them by Ballot the Vice President.

The Congress may determine the Time of chusing the Electors, and the Day on which they shall give their Votes; which Day shall be the same throughout the United States.

No Person except a natural born Citizen, or a Citizen of the United States, at the time of the Adoption of this Constitution, shall be eligible to the Office of President; neither shall any Person be eligible to that Office who shall not have attained to the Age of thirty five Years, and been fourteen Years a Resident within the United States.

In Case of the Removal of the President from Office, or of his Death, Resignation, or Inability to discharge the Powers and Duties of the said Office, the Same shall devolve on the Vice President, and the Congress may by Law provide for the Case of Removal, Death, Resignation or Inability, both of the President and Vice President, declaring what Officer shall then act as President, and such Officer shall act accordingly, until the Disability be removed, or a President shall be elected.

The President shall, at stated Times, receive for his Services, a Compensation, which shall neither be encreased nor diminished during the Period for which he shall have been elected, and he shall not receive within that Period any other Emolument from the United States, or any of them.

Before he enter on the Execution of his Office, he shall take the following Oath or Affirmation:–"I do solemnly swear (or affirm) that I will faithfully execute the Office of President of the United States, and will to the best of my Ability, preserve, protect and defend the Constitution of the United States."

Section 2

The President shall be Commander in Chief of the Army and Navy of the United States, and of the Militia of the several States, when called into the actual Service of the United States; he may require the Opinion, in writing, of the principal Officer in each of the executive Departments, upon any Subject relating to the Duties of their respective

Offices, and he shall have Power to grant Reprieves and Pardons for Offences against the United States, except in Cases of Impeachment.

He shall have Power, by and with the Advice and Consent of the Senate, to make Treaties, provided two thirds of the Senators present concur; and he shall nominate, and by and with the Advice and Consent of the Senate, shall appoint Ambassadors, other public Ministers and Consuls, Judges of the supreme Court, and all other Officers of the United States, whose Appointments are not herein otherwise provided for, and which shall be established by Law: but the Congress may by Law vest the Appointment of such inferior Officers, as they think proper, in the President alone, in the Courts of Law, or in the Heads of Departments.

The President shall have Power to fill up all Vacancies that may happen during the Recess of the Senate, by granting Commissions which shall expire at the End of their next Session.

Section 3

He shall from time to time give to the Congress Information of the State of the Union, and recommend to their Consideration such Measures as he shall judge necessary and expedient; he may, on extraordinary Occasions, convene both Houses, or either of them, and in Case of Disagreement between them, with Respect to the Time of Adjournment, he may adjourn them to such Time as he shall think proper; he shall receive Ambassadors and other public Ministers; he shall take Care that the Laws be faithfully executed, and shall Commission all the Officers of the United States.

Section 4

The President, Vice President and all civil Officers of the United States, shall be removed from Office on Impeachment for, and

Conviction of, Treason, Bribery, or other high Crimes and Misdemeanors.

Article III

Section 1

The judicial Power of the United States, shall be vested in one supreme Court, and in such inferior Courts as the Congress may from time to time ordain and establish. The Judges, both of the supreme and inferior Courts, shall hold their Offices during good Behaviour, and shall, at stated Times, receive for their Services, a Compensation, which shall not be diminished during their Continuance in Office.

Section 2

The judicial Power shall extend to all Cases, in Law and Equity, arising under this Constitution, the Laws of the United States, and Treaties made, or which shall be made, under their Authority;–to all Cases affecting Ambassadors, other public Ministers and Consuls;–to all Cases of admiralty and maritime Jurisdiction;–to Controversies to which the United States shall be a Party;–to Controversies between two or more States;–between a State and Citizens of another State;–between Citizens of different States;–between Citizens of the same State claiming Lands under Grants of different States, and between a State, or the Citizens thereof, and foreign States, Citizens or Subjects.

In all Cases affecting Ambassadors, other public Ministers and Consuls, and those in which a State shall be Party, the supreme Court shall have original Jurisdiction. In all the other Cases before mentioned, the supreme Court shall have appellate Jurisdiction, both as to Law and Fact, with such Exceptions, and under such Regulations as the Congress shall make.

The Trial of all Crimes, except in Cases of Impeachment; shall be by Jury; and such Trial shall be held in the State where the said Crimes shall have been committed; but when not committed within any State, the Trial shall be at such Place or Places as the Congress may by Law have directed.

Section 3

Treason against the United States, shall consist only in levying War against them, or in adhering to their Enemies, giving them Aid and Comfort. No Person shall be convicted of Treason unless on the Testimony of two Witnesses to the same overt Act, or on Confession in open Court.

The Congress shall have Power to declare the Punishment of Treason, but no Attainder of Treason shall work Corruption of Blood, or Forfeiture except during the Life of the Person attainted.

Article IV

Section 1

Full Faith and Credit shall be given in each State to the public Acts, Records, and judicial Proceedings of every other State. And the Congress may by general Laws prescribe the Manner in which such Acts, Records and Proceedings shall be proved, and the Effect thereof.

Section 2

The Citizens of each State shall be entitled to all Privileges and Immunities of Citizens in the several States.

A Person charged in any State with Treason, Felony, or other Crime, who shall flee from Justice, and be found in another State, shall on Demand of the executive Authority of the State from which he fled, be delivered up, to be removed to the State having Jurisdiction of the Crime.

No Person held to Service or Labour in one State, under the Laws thereof, escaping into another, shall, in Consequence of any Law or Regulation therein, be discharged from such Service or Labour, but shall be delivered up on Claim of the Party to whom such Service or Labour may be due.

Section 3

New States may be admitted by the Congress into this Union; but no new State shall be formed or erected within the Jurisdiction of any other State; nor any State be formed by the Junction of two or more States, or Parts of States, without the Consent of the Legislatures of the States concerned as well as of the Congress.

The Congress shall have Power to dispose of and make all needful Rules and Regulations respecting the Territory or other Property belonging to the United States; and nothing in this Constitution shall be so construed as to Prejudice any Claims of the United States, or of any particular State.

Section 4

The United States shall guarantee to every State in this Union a Republican Form of Government, and shall protect each of them against Invasion; and on Application of the Legislature, or of the Executive (when the Legislature cannot be convened) against domestic Violence.

Article V

The Congress, whenever two thirds of both Houses shall deem it necessary, shall propose Amendments to this Constitution, or, on the

Application of the Legislatures of two thirds of the several States, shall call a Convention for proposing Amendments, which, in either Case, shall be valid to all Intents and Purposes, as Part of this Constitution, when ratified by the Legislatures of three fourths of the several States, or by Conventions in three fourths thereof, as the one or the other Mode of Ratification may be proposed by the Congress; Provided that no Amendment which may be made prior to the Year One thousand eight hundred and eight shall in any Manner affect the first and fourth Clauses in the Ninth Section of the first Article; and that no State, without its Consent, shall be deprived of its equal Suffrage in the Senate.

Article VI

All Debts contracted and Engagements entered into, before the Adoption of this Constitution, shall be as valid against the United States under this Constitution, as under the Confederation.

This Constitution, and the Laws of the United States which shall be made in Pursuance thereof; and all Treaties made, or which shall be made, under the Authority of the United States, shall be the supreme Law of the Land; and the Judges in every State shall be bound thereby, any Thing in the Constitution or Laws of any State to the Contrary notwithstanding.

The Senators and Representatives before mentioned, and the Members of the several State Legislatures, and all executive and judicial Officers, both of the United States and of the several States, shall be bound by Oath or Affirmation, to support this Constitution; but no religious Test shall ever be required as a Qualification to any Office or public Trust under the United States.

Resources

General Legislative Resources

- **Glossary of Legislative Terms**
  - *Description:* Comprehensive glossary for understanding legislative terminology.
  - *URL:* https://www.ncsl.org/resources/details/glossary-of-legislative-terms
- **National Conference of State Legislatures (NCSL)**
  - *Description:* Resources and tools supporting state legislatures and their work.
  - *URL:* https://www.ncsl.org/our-work

Professional Organizations

- **American Association of Political Consultants**
  - *Description:* Professional association for political consultants.
  - *URL:* https://theaapc.org/

- **National Institute for Lobbying & Ethics**
  - ○ *Description:* Provides lobbying ethics guidelines, professional development, and certification.
  - ○ *URL:* https://www.lobbyinginstitute.com/
- **American Political Science Association**
  - ○ *Description:* Association for political science professionals and researchers.
  - ○ *URL:* https://apsanet.org/

Transparency & Public Policy Resources

- **OpenSecrets**
  - ○ *Description:* Research and transparency platform tracking money in politics and its effect on elections and policy.
  - ○ *URL:* https://www.opensecrets.org/
- **Vote Smart**
  - ○ *Description:* Provides unbiased information on candidates and elected officials.
  - ○ *URL:* https://justfacts.votesmart.org/
- **Pew Research Center**
  - ○ *Description:* Nonpartisan fact tank informing the public about issues, attitudes, and trends shaping the world.
  - ○ *URL:* https://www.pewresearch.org/

Foundational Documents

- **Charters of Freedom**
  - ○ *Description:* Access to foundational documents such as the Declaration of Independence, Constitution, and Bill of Rights.
  - ○ *URL:* https://www.archives.gov/founding-docs

Media & Monitoring Platforms

- **MeltWater**
  - *Description:* Media, social, and consumer intelligence platform.
  - *URL:* https://explore.meltwater.com/
- **Google Alerts & Social Mention**
  - *Description:* Free tools to track mentions of key issues, clients, or stakeholders.
  - *URL:* Google Alerts | Social Mention

Education Platforms

- **Coursera**
  - *Description:* Online education platform offering courses on various subjects, including government relations.
  - *URL:* https://www.coursera.org/
- **EdX**
  - *Description:* For-profit online education platform providing access to university-level courses.
  - *URL:* https://www.edx.org/

Legislative & Public Information Platforms

- **LegiStorm**
  - *Description:* Platform for accessing information on congressional staff, salaries, and biographies.
  - *URL:* https://info.legistorm.com/
- **Quorum**
  - *Description:* Public information platform with legislative tracking and advocacy tools.
  - *URL:* https://www.quorum.us/

- **FiscalNote**
  - *Description:* Platform for public information access, legislative analysis, and stakeholder engagement.
  - *URL:* https://fiscalnote.com/

Productivity & Work Management Tools

- **Trello**
  - *Description:* Project management platform.
  - *URL:* https://trello.com/
- **Slack**
  - *Description:* Work management and productivity tool, including AI-powered collaboration features.
  - *URL:* https://slack.com/

AI Writing & Creative Platforms

- **ChatGBT 4.0**
  - *Description:* ChatGPT 4.0 is an advanced AI language model designed to understand and generate human-like text, enabling natural conversations, content creation, problem-solving, and more, with improved accuracy, creativity, and contextual understanding compared to previous versions.
  - *URL:* https://chat.openai.com.
- **Jasper AI**
  - *Description:* AI-powered writing assistant for generating content across blogs, social media, and marketing.
  - *URL:* https://www.jasper.ai/

- **Adobe Firefly**
  - ○ *Description:* AI-driven suite within Adobe Creative Cloud for generating images and text effects.
  - ○ *URL:* https://www.adobe.com/sensei/generative-ai/firefly.html
- **Runway**
  - ○ *Description:* AI platform offering tools for video editing and generation.
  - ○ *URL:* https://runwayml.com/

State-Specific Legislative Resources

- **State Legislature Websites**
  - ○ *Description:* Websites for tracking bills, voting records, committee reports, and other legislative activities on a state-by-state basis.
- **State Lobbying Associations**
  - ○ *Description:* Many states, including Colorado, have lobbying associations that provide specific state-focused resources, networking opportunities, and educational content.

The Kyle Group

Trusted Name in Government Affairs

Who We Are:

The Kyle Group is a leading government affairs firm that provides expert lobbying, legislative training, and public speaking services. With more than forty-four years of state experience, we represent associations and businesses before the legislature and regulatory agencies, ensuring their voices are heard where they matter most.

Our Services:

1. Expert Lobbying Services:

We leverage decades of experience and deep connections within the legislative process to advance your interests effectively. Our lobbying services include:

2. Legislative Training:

We believe in empowering organizations and individuals to engage in the legislative process. Our training programs are designed to give participants the tools they need to succeed in government affairs.

3. Public Speaking & Keynote Addresses:

Our team provides insightful, engaging presentations on government relations, lobbying strategies, and public policy. We bring our wealth of experience to your event and deliver clear, actionable insights.

Why Choose The Kyle Group?

Proven Track Record: Over four decades of experience with a reputation for delivering results.

Personalized Approach: We take the time to understand your unique needs and tailor our services accordingly.

Deep Legislative Knowledge: A comprehensive understanding of state political landscape.

Personal Touch: We are a hands-on firm working with you daily to obtain your legislative goals.

About the Author

Henry Kyle is a seasoned state lobbyist with over forty years of experience representing associations and businesses of all sizes before state legislatures. Known as a master of the art of political influence, Henry has dedicated his career to advancing the interests of his clients while navigating the complexities of policy and power. A lifelong advocate for accountability and citizen engagement, he has seen firsthand the impact of skilled lobbying on shaping legislation and fostering transparency in government. Henry lives in Arvada, Colorado, a suburb of Denver, with his wife, Susan. Together, they have built a close-knit family that includes their four children—Jeff, Kristen, Brandon, and Cody—along with ten grandchildren and three great-grandchildren. *Hardball Advocacy: Secrets of the Lobby* reflects Henry's professional legacy, his passion for advocacy, and the values guiding his work and life.

To Purchase your copy or copies of "Hardball Advocacy: Secrets of the Lobby." Go to our website.

Contact Us Today:
Phone: 303-263-5422
Email: Ckyle@TheKyleGroup.com
Website: www.Thekylegroup.com

The Kyle Group welcomes any and all suggestions for the enhancement of our book. Send your thoughts and comment to: Ckyle@thekylegroup.com.

Let The Kyle Group be your trusted partner in navigating the complex world of government affairs!